952

D0099680

Withdrawn

COUNTRIES
OF THE
WORLD

Japan

Gareth Stevens Publishing
MILWAUKEE

Harlinah Whyte has a degree in Japanese language and Japanese Studies. She spent a year at a Tokyo university and has also worked in Japan as an English teacher and translator. When she's not writing books, she produces Internet websites for a living.

Written by
HARLINAH WHYTE

Edited by
AUDREY LIM SUAT HUI

Designed by
LYNN CHIN

Picture research by
SUSAN JANE MANUEL

First published in North America in 1998 by
Gareth Stevens Publishing
1555 North RiverCenter Drive, Suite 201
Milwaukee, Wisconsin 53212 USA

For a free color catalog describing
Gareth Stevens' list of high-quality books
and multimedia programs, call
1-800-542-2595 (USA) or
1-800-461-9120 (CANADA)
Gareth Stevens Publishing's
Fax: (414) 225-0377.
See our catalog, on the World Wide Web:
http://gsinc.com

© **TIMES EDITIONS PTE LTD 1998**
Originated and designed by
Times Books International
an imprint of Times Editions Pte Ltd
Times Centre, 1 New Industrial Road
Singapore 536196
http://www.timesone.com.sg/te

Library of Congress Cataloging-in-Publication Data
Whyte, Harlinah.
Japan / by Harlinah Whyte.
p. cm. —(Countries of the world)
Includes bibliographical references and index.
Summary: Provides an overview of the country of Japan, its geography, history, government, people, culture, and social issues.
ISBN 0-8368-2126-2 (lib. bdg.)
1. Japan—Juvenile literature. 2. Japan—Pictorial works—Juvenile literature. [1. Japan.] I. Title.
II. Series: Countries of the world (Milwaukee, Wis.)
DS806.W49   1998
952—DC21   97-42540

Printed in Singapore

1 2 3 4 5 6 7 8 9 02 01 00 99 98

Contents

5 AN OVERVIEW OF JAPAN

6 Geography
10 History
16 Government and the Economy
20 People and Lifestyle
28 Language and Literature
30 Arts
34 Leisure and Festivals
40 Food

43 A CLOSER LOOK AT JAPAN

44 Ainu, the Native People of Japan
46 Architecture in Japan
48 Atomic Bombs
50 Baths and Hot Springs
52 Comics in Japan
54 Etiquette
56 Gardens
58 Inventions
60 Kimonos
62 Natural Disasters
64 Pollution
66 Sumo Wrestling
68 Sushi
70 Women in Japan
72 Yakuza

75 RELATIONS WITH NORTH AMERICA

For More Information …
86 Full-color map
88 Black-and-white reproducible map
90 Japan at a Glance
92 Glossary
94 Books, Videos, Web Sites
95 Index

AN OVERVIEW OF JAPAN

Welcome to Japan, the Land of the Rising Sun! The Japanese call their country *Nihon* (nee-hon), which means "source of the sun." This name dates from the early days of Japanese history. Japanese culture is thousands of years old. Over the centuries, the Japanese have learned and adapted new technologies and ideas from other countries, but they have never forgotten their unique history and traditions. Today, Japanese society continues to combine ancient traditions and modern innovations.

Join us as we explore this exciting country. We will start with an overview of Japan and its people so as to help us better understand Japanese culture. Then, we will take a closer look at some of Japan's customs and social issues and what makes Japan unique!

Opposite: **The busy streets of Tokyo.**

Below: **Despite its unique traditions, Western culture is pervasive in Japan. Like children in Western countries, these two youngsters are enjoying their soft drinks.**

THE FLAG OF JAPAN

The Japanese flag, known as *Hinomaru* (hee-no-mah-roo), "the circle of the sun," was confirmed as the national flag in 1870. It has a white background with a red circle in the center. The circle represents the sun, an important symbol of Japanese nationalism. Legends say that the Japanese emperor is descended from the sun goddess, Amaterasu. The Japanese also call their country *Nihon* or *Nippon*, which means "source of the sun." From this comes the nickname for Japan: "Land of the Rising Sun."

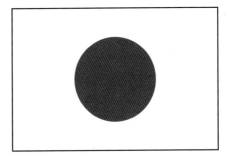

Geography

The Land

Japan consists of a chain of islands in the Pacific Ocean off the northeastern coast of the Asian continent. The country stretches 1,865 miles (3,000 kilometers) from north to south. At its widest point, it is only about 250 miles (402 km) wide. There are four large islands — Honshu, Hokkaido, Shikoku, and Kyushu — and over one thousand smaller islands. To Japan's west lie its nearest neighbors, China and Korea. Far to the east, across the Pacific Ocean, are the United States and Canada.

Japan has dramatic coastlines and spectacular mountains. More than three-quarters of the country is mountainous. The mountains are covered with dense forests, and rivers run through the mountain valleys. Farms and houses cannot be built on the steep slopes, so most people live along the narrow coastal plains. The largest area of flat land is the Kanto Plain on Honshu. Tokyo, the capital, and Yokohama, Japan's second largest city, are located here. Osaka, Kyoto, Nagoya, and Kobe — all major cities — are also located along Honshu's coastal plains.

NATURAL DISASTERS

The worst earthquake in modern Japanese history occurred in 1923. It is known as the Great Kanto Earthquake because it was centered in the Kanto Plain. The earthquake devastated the Tokyo area, and over one hundred thousand people died. Many of the deaths were caused by fires that roared through the city after the earthquake.

(A Closer Look, page 62)

Below: This view of the Japanese Alps is breathtaking. The Alps are formed by the Akaishi, Kiso, and Hida ranges. People enjoy going to these ranges to ski.

Japan was formed millions of years ago by violent movements in the earth's crust. A mountain range was pushed up out of the sea, and the peaks of this range form the islands of Japan. These land movements continue even today, causing volcanic eruptions and earthquakes.

Above: **Many people climb Mount Fuji through the night in order to reach the summit at dawn and greet the rising sun.**

Mount Fuji

Mount Fuji is recognizable throughout the world as a symbol of Japan. This spectacular peak is a volcano, although it has not erupted since 1707. The mountain is particularly beautiful in winter and spring, when it is capped with snow. The Japanese consider Mount Fuji a symbol of the beauty of their land. It has been the subject of paintings and poetry for hundreds of years. Every summer, thousands of people climb Mount Fuji. For some, it is a spiritual pilgrimage; for others, a sporting challenge. There are no trees on Mount Fuji, so the climb is rocky and tedious. However, there is a special sense of achievement when the climber reaches the top.

Seasons

Japan's climate varies greatly from north to south. Northern Japan experiences long, harsh winters. Icy winds blow from the Asian continent, bringing heavy snowfall. In Sapporo, average winter temperatures are 23° Fahrenheit (-5° Centigrade). However, summers are mild, with temperatures averaging 68° F (20° C).

The central and southern areas of Japan experience a short rainy period in the early summer. Summers are hot and humid. In September, tropical cyclones bring heavy rainfall and sometimes cause flooding and damage to houses and crops.

Farther south, the winters are milder and the summers even hotter. In Okinawa, in the Ryukyu Islands, the average summer temperature is 82° F (28° C). It never gets very cold this far south; the average winter temperature is a comfortable 59° F (15° C).

Above: **Maple trees turn beautiful colors in autumn.**

GARDENS

The Japanese appreciation of nature can be seen in their unique tradition of landscape gardening. Gardens are carefully designed to enhance the natural beauty of a site and to create a peaceful and harmonious place.
(*A Closer Look, page 56*)

Left: **When the cherry trees bloom, people flock to parks and the countryside to look at the white and pink blossoms and enjoy the spring weather.**

Cherry Blossoms

The four seasons are an important theme in Japanese culture and art. The beginning of spring is especially important, as this is the time when the cherry trees flower. Cherry blossoms last only three days before they fall. The Japanese believe that the blossoms are like life — beautiful, but passing quickly.

Television programs and newspapers report when the first blossoms appear in southern Japan. As the weather warms up and the blossoms appear farther north, the newspapers give constant updates on the best blossom-viewing sites.

Plants and Animals

Two-thirds of Japan is covered with forest, making it one of the most forested countries in the world. These forests have managed to survive the industrialization of Japan because they grow on steep, inaccessible mountain ranges.

Japan has a number of unique animals, such as the Asiatic brown bear of Honshu, Shikoku, and Kyushu. Other land mammals include wild boars, badgers, and deer. Japan's native birds are mostly waterbirds, such as gulls and cranes. There are also over one hundred and fifty species of songbirds. The Sea of Japan supports a large variety of sea life.

Above: **The Japanese macaque can be found on Honshu, Shikoku, and Kyushu. It grows to about 2 feet (61 centimeters) in length and has a short tail. Its thick, furry coat enables it to survive the cold winters.**

9

History

The first settlers in Japan probably came from Siberia. Later, settlers from China and Korea migrated to southwestern Japan and, moving north, mixed with the original people. Over many centuries, families organized themselves into clans and fought each other for control of land. By A.D. 300, the Yamato clan had become dominant. This clan claimed they were descended from the sun goddess, Amaterasu. They called their leader "emperor." This line of emperors has continued to the present day.

In the sixth century, ambassadors visited China and brought back many Chinese ideas, including their religion and philosophy.

ARCHITECTURE IN JAPAN

Feudal lords built fortified castles during the sixteenth and seventeenth centuries. Himeji Castle is thought to be the most beautiful castle in Japan. It was built in 1557. Other castles, such as Nagoya Castle and Osaka Castle, were destroyed during World War II. They have been replaced by concrete reconstructions — Nagoya Castle even has an elevator!
(A Closer Look, page 46)

Left: Feudal wars not only resulted in loss of lives, they also led to the destruction of great architecture. The Todaiji temple at Nara, built between 745 and 752, was completely destroyed by a Taira general for supporting the Minamoto clan. It was later rebuilt in a newer style.

The Heian Era and Subsequent Civil War

In 794, Kyoto (then known as Heian) became Japan's capital. During the Heian era, political power was held by the powerful and corrupt Fujiwara clan. The Fujiwaras were eventually ousted by the Taira clan, who were in turn defeated by the Minamoto (or Genji) clan. Although the emperor remained in Kyoto, real power shifted to the Minamoto stronghold at Kamakura. Minamoto Yoritomo became *shogun* (sho-gen), that is, military leader, and the most powerful lord in Japan. However, the fighting continued. Hundreds of years of civil war followed as feudal lords fought for control of the land.

Above: **Buddhism, arts, and samurai culture flourished at Kamakura for many centuries. This painting was done during the Kamakura period.**

Centuries of Isolation

Japan was finally united in the sixteenth century when a lord named Tokugawa Ieyasu became shogun of the whole country. The Tokugawa shogunate believed that foreign contact was bad for Japan. In 1637, foreigners were expelled from Japan, and Japanese people were banned from traveling overseas. For over two centuries, Japan was almost completely isolated from the rest of the world.

The End of Japanese Seclusion

Japan's seclusion ended when American ships arrived at Japan in 1854. The shogun was forced to open trade with the West. Soon, Japan was trading with the United States, Britain, Russia, and the Netherlands.

The Tokugawa shogunate was overthrown in 1868, and the emperor ruled Japan once again. Under Emperor Meiji, the Japanese modernized their country. The strict social classes of the Tokugawa era were abolished. Japanese students were sent to study in the West. Foreign experts were invited to Japan to teach the Japanese about Western technologies. The Japanese introduced railroads, communication systems, a constitution, and a public school system. A modern army and navy were also created.

Japan at War

By 1900, Japan was the most advanced nation in Asia. After defeating China in the First Sino-Japanese War (1894–95), the Japanese defeated Russia in 1905, surprising Europe.

Above: Japanese naval officers march in parade. Despite its post-World War II constitution, which states that Japan will not go to war, Japan has a well-equipped military force called the Self Defense Force. During the Gulf War, Japan assisted U.S. and international forces by sending navy vessels to clear explosive mines from the sea. Although Japan did not engage in combat, many people felt that the constitution had been breached.

Japan continued to expand its power in the region, taking over Korea in 1910. In 1937, Japan went to war against China again. In the following years, the Japanese took control of much of eastern Asia, as far south as Indonesia and New Guinea.

On December 7, 1941, Japan entered World War II by bombing the U.S. naval base at Pearl Harbor in Hawaii. The battle in the Pacific raged for over three and a half years. Many of Japan's major cities were bombed and destroyed by fire. Then, in August 1945, the United States dropped two atomic bombs on the Japanese cities of Hiroshima and Nagasaki. Japan surrendered, and the American army took control. The Americans remained in Japan until 1952. Japan was devastated by the war. In addition to the loss of life, crops, houses, and factories were destroyed, and many people were left homeless and starving. The United States and other countries helped Japan rebuild its cities and economy. A new democratic constitution was created, which stated that Japan would never again go to war.

During the 1960s, Japan's economy underwent an amazing recovery. Although Japan's economic growth has slowed in the 1990s, its economy remains strong.

THE ATOMIC BOMBS

Hiroshima's and Nagasaki's bombings are remembered with horror because a single weapon was used to kill so many people. More than fifty years after the bombings, people still debate whether it was right to use atomic bombs to end the war.

(*A Closer Look*, page 48)

Below: In 1947, Emperor Hirohito (1901–1989) rode in an open car during a trip to Osaka. It was the first time a Japanese emperor had done so.

Emperor Meiji (1852–1912)

Emperor Meiji oversaw Japan's golden era of modernization. He was born Prince Mutsuhito and became emperor when he was only fifteen, taking the name Meiji, meaning "enlightened government." In 1868, soon after he became emperor, the Tokugawa shogunate was overthrown and a new government headed by Emperor Meiji was formed. This national revolution is known as the Meiji Restoration. Meiji was the first emperor to reside in Tokyo. He became an influential force in the government and an important symbol of national unity. Meiji was dedicated to the modernization of Japan. The Meiji shrine in the center of Tokyo was built in his honor.

Above: **This is what Tokugawa Ieyasu looked like. His exercise of patience was one of the ways he acquired more power.**

Murasaki Shikibu (978–1026)

Murasaki Shikibu wrote *The Tale of Genji*. This novel, a detailed and realistic examination of life in the Heian court, is one of the greatest works of Japanese literature. Murasaki's real name is unknown — she took the name "Murasaki" from a character in the book. She lived in the royal court, where she was an attendant of the empress. Her novel and her personal diary show her sensitivity to human emotions and her love of nature.

Tokugawa Ieyasu (1543–1616)

Tokugawa Ieyasu united Japan after centuries of civil war and founded the city of Tokyo. He was a skillful military commander and a shrewd judge of character. He increased his power through clever planning and alliances with other lords. While others fought for power, he watched carefully and gradually increased his own lands. In 1600, he defeated his major rival in the battle of Sekigahara and became the shogun of all of Japan. He established Edo (Tokyo) and maintained his power through strict laws. The Tokugawas ruled Japan for over two hundred and sixty years.

Minamoto Yoritomo (1147–1199)

Minamoto Yoritomo was Japan's first shogun (military leader). He was a brilliant political strategist. When he became shogun in 1192, he established a feudal system that continued until the nineteenth century. Under this system, the emperor had no real power and warriors formed the highest social class. Minamoto established his capital at Kamakura.

Opposite: **Emperor Meiji in military dress. Although the Meiji Restoration brought about great changes, the lives of ordinary Japanese did not change drastically. Hardship remained in most of the rural areas.**

Government and the Economy

Government

After World War II, Japan became a constitutional monarchy with a new constitution. Hirohito, emperor from 1926 to 1989, remained the symbolic ruler of the nation, but he had no power in the government. When he died in 1989, his son Akihito became emperor.

The Japanese constitution is based on the principles of sovereignty of the people, respect for human rights, and pacifism. The constitution was written immediately after the war, and it includes an important clause that forever renounces war and aggression as a means of settling international disputes.

Japan has a democratic government. All people over the age of twenty have the right to vote. The head of government is the prime minister. The Japanese do not elect their leader directly, as in the United States. They vote for a political party, and the

Below: **The National Diet Building is an imposing structure in Tokyo.**

16

Left: **This political hopeful was making the rounds during the 1995 governor's election in Tokyo.**

majority party chooses a prime minister from among its members. The strongest political party in Japan is the Liberal Democratic Party (LDP), which held power continuously from 1955 until 1993. In 1997, the LDP shared power with two other parties. The prime minister was Hashimoto Ryutaro.

The national government administers matters affecting the whole country, such as the national economy, foreign relations, defense, and the school curriculum. The prime minister is assisted by a cabinet of ministers, chosen from among the members of the national legislature, called the Diet. The Diet has two chambers: the House of Representatives and the House of Councillors. The members of the Diet vote on laws for the country. The Diet building is located in Tokyo, the capital city.

On a regional level, Japan is divided into forty-seven prefectures, each with a governor and an assembly of elected representatives. Eleven major cities have similar governments. Beneath the prefectural and city governments are about three thousand municipal authorities that look after administrative matters at a city, ward, town, or village level. They maintain parks, run elementary and middle schools, operate health services, and collect garbage. Each municipality has a single-chamber legislature. Assembly men and women are elected directly by the local residents for a period of four years.

Below: **A policeman on duty at his "police box." This is a single-room police station where people go for information or to report lost items. There is a police box in every neighborhood.**

Economic Development

Japan is one of the world's economic superpowers. In a hundred years it has developed from a poor, farming country to a rich industrial country. Since the 1950s, Japan's strong economy has been built on its exports.

Japan has few natural resources, so much of its energy sources and raw materials are imported. Japan's industries use the raw materials to make manufactured goods, such as ships, cars, motorcycles, cameras, computers, televisions, stereo equipment, and musical instruments. Most of these goods are then exported to other countries. Motor vehicles and other manufactured goods make up over 99 percent of Japan's exports. One-third of these goods are exported to the United States.

Japanese companies invest large sums of money to develop new, high quality products. Labor and other costs are high in Japan, so many Japanese companies have set up factories in neighboring areas such as Taiwan, Malaysia, South Korea, and Hong Kong, where costs are lower. As manufacturing jobs decrease, more Japanese people are being employed in service-related industries, such as research, communications, and banking.

Above: **Japanese companies are well-managed, and the workers are skilled and loyal. This worker is making printer ribbons for Hitachi Heavy Metals.**

INVENTIONS

The Japanese are constantly searching for ways to improve their lives. They have invented things that are small and easy to carry around. A peculiar invention is the electronic Tamagotchi — an electronic "pet" designed for city people. City people who adore animals can now play with their "pet" chick.

(A Closer Look, page 58)

Agriculture

Agricultural products and minerals make up less than 1 percent of Japan's exports. The most important crop is rice. Because farms in Japan are small, large modern machinery cannot be used, and the rice is very expensive to produce. Until 1993, Japanese farmers were protected by a law that banned imports of cheaper rice from other countries. Even though Japanese rice was very expensive, the Japanese did not want to be dependent on other countries for their staple food. However, a wet summer in 1993 caused the failure of the rice crop, and Japan was forced to open its market to foreign rice growers.

Energy

Japan's energy comes mainly from oil and coal, most of which are imported. In order to reduce its dependence on oil and coal, Japan is developing nuclear power stations. The power stations are fueled by uranium, a radioactive mineral. To run a nuclear power plant, only a small amount of uranium is needed, instead of thousands of tons of oil or coal. However, nuclear power plants produce highly dangerous waste products that remain toxic for tens of thousands of years.

POLLUTION

Japan's economic growth has been a double-edged sword. Although it has raised Japanese living standards, it has also damaged the environment. This damage includes air and water pollution. Laws have been introduced to help solve these problems.
(A Closer Look, page 64)

Below: **Japan's farms are very small, usually only 2–5 acres (1–2 hectares). These farmers are harvesting their crop.**

People and Lifestyle

Who lives in Japan?

About 125 million people live in Japan, making it the seventh most populous country in the world. Most Japanese are descended from people who migrated from the Asian continent thousands of years ago. Since that time, there has been very little immigration. In general, the Japanese have straight black hair and dark brown or black eyes.

Although ethnic Japanese form the vast majority of the population, there are several minority groups. One of these is the *Ainu* (eye-noo), who were living in the Japanese islands before the first immigrants arrived from the Asian mainland. Today, most of Japan's Ainu population lives in Hokkaido. The ethnic Japanese, together with the Ainu, make up 99.2 percent of the Japanese population.

About 0.6 percent of the population are Koreans. The remaining 0.2 percent of the population in Japan includes people from China and other countries.

THE AINU

The Ainu are physically different from the ethnic Japanese. They have fair skin, round eyes, and more body hair. Ainu men traditionally grew long beards. Most of Japan's Ainu population live in Hokkaido.
(A Closer Look, page 44)

Below: **Holding two fingers up in a "V" is a popular pose for photographs in Japan. The population of Japan is not very racially mixed. Most Japanese are descended from people who migrated from the Asian continent thousands of years ago. Since that time, there has been very little immigration.**

Types of Buildings

Due to Japan's mountainous terrain, over 90 percent of the Japanese live on the coastal plains. The plains on the Pacific side of Honshu are among the most densely populated areas in the world, with 36,000 people to every square mile (14,000 per square km). More than three-quarters of the population live in large cities, such as Tokyo, Yokohama, and Osaka. Due to the risk of earthquakes, Japanese cities do not have many skyscrapers. Instead, the business districts are filled with medium-rise buildings, while the residential areas form a dense, sprawling ring of low-rise buildings around the city center.

Japanese Homes

Japan's economic success has improved living standards in the last forty years. Japanese homes are comfortable but small by Western standards. A middle-class family of four shares two or three rooms, plus a kitchen and bathroom. The kitchen often has a Western-style table and chairs, where meals are eaten. The rooms double as living areas and bedrooms. At night, the family sleeps on bedding called *futon* (foo-ton), which are laid out on the floor. In the morning, the futon are stored in a cupboard.

Above: **Japanese rooms have smooth *tatami* (tah-tah-mee) floors made of tightly woven rice stalks. A low table is placed in the center of the room for people to sit around.**

ETIQUETTE

There are many formal social customs in Japan. One must behave a certain way when meeting another person, exchanging name cards, or giving gifts.
(A Closer Look, page 54)

Belonging to a Group

In Japan, it is important for a person to be part of a group —
whether family, school, company, or club. North Americans value
individuality — the ability to express your own ideas and make
your own way in the world. This way of living seems lonely and
selfish to many Japanese. The Japanese believe that a well-
balanced person is able to work closely with other people, blend
in, and not disrupt the group harmony. Within this group
structure, people can express their own personalities.

Growing Up

Throughout their lives, the Japanese define themselves according
to their group relationships. Small children are part of the family
group. They are protected, coddled, and never left alone. Parents
allow them to be noisy and naughty because social rules do not
apply to them yet.

As soon as children start school, they become part of the
school community. They are required to obey the rules of the
group and fit in with the other children. This expectation
continues throughout school and work life.

Above: **Japanese teens
enjoy the treats of an
amusement park. Being
part of a group is
important even when
having fun.**

Opposite: **Women
shoulder heavy
responsibilities in
the household, looking
after the household
finances, as well as
taking care of their
children.**

Within the groups, there are strict hierarchies based on age and experience. Younger students must be respectful to older students. Company employees are promoted according to how long they have been with the company.

Roles for Men and Women

Men are expected to work hard and support their family. The typical image of the Japanese man is the "salaryman," who works long hours at his company, entertains guests after work, and comes home late at night. This tiring lifestyle is a reality for many men in Japan's cities.

Many single women work, but most give up their jobs when they get married. Married women are traditionally expected to remain at home to look after their family. Women handle the household finances and give their husband a weekly allowance. They are also responsible for overseeing their children's education. Once their children have finished school, women have a lot of leisure time and can attend self-enrichment classes during the day.

WOMEN IN JAPAN

The earliest Japanese records show that women once held positions of authority in Japan. People worshiped powerful goddesses. Queens were mediators between warring tribes. The introduction of Chinese culture in the sixth century brought new social structures and attitudes to Japan. Men began to dominate public life, and the status of women declined.
(*A Closer Look, page 70*)

Education

The Japanese education system is very competitive. Advancing to each level involves passing tough examinations. The most difficult examinations are for university entrance. Universities are ranked according to their quality and prestige. Graduates of the top universities are assured of excellent jobs in the government and major companies, so competition for places at these universities is fierce. Those who fail the first time may keep studying and try again the following year. After finishing high school, some students study for several years just to pass the university entrance exam. Once they enter the university, students do not have to work as hard, and few fail.

Left: **In the Japanese education system, advancing to each level involves going through a round of tough examinations. These two girls in their graduation** *yukata* **(yoo-kah-tah) have certainly come a long way!**

School Life

The Japanese school year is long — 240 days a year. It runs from April to March, with six weeks of vacation in the summer. Classes are held Monday through Friday, plus a half day on Saturday. The school curriculum and textbooks are set by the Ministry of Education, and teachers must follow the set lessons. On any given day, twelve-year-old students all over Japan study the same page of the same textbook. Core subjects include mathematics, science, social studies, Japanese, art, music, physical education, morals (the study of correct behavior), and calligraphy (the art of writing Japanese). Japanese children are taught to respect their teachers and to work together with other students to take care of their school. Students are responsible for cleaning the classrooms, halls, bathrooms, and tending the garden.

Cram Schools and Examination Hell

From as early as elementary school, many students go to private "cram schools" in the evenings and on weekends. The cram schools help students do the extra work necessary to survive "examination hell" — studying for entrance exams. In addition, students take home several hours of homework every day. Many students take other private lessons, such as piano or swimming.

Above: **Most young Japanese learn to live with their heavy study workload. However, the Japanese media have reported a growing number of students who drop out of school or commit suicide because they are unable to cope with the pressures of the education system.**

Religion

The main religions in Japan are Buddhism and Shinto. Most people say they are not religious — they do not go to the temple or pray regularly. However, Buddhist and Shinto rituals are mixed into many Japanese traditions.

Shinto

Shinto, meaning "way of the gods," originated in Japan in prehistoric times. The early Japanese believed that gods or spirits existed all around them in nature. By worshiping these spirits, they tried to live in harmony with nature. They also honored their ancestors and national heroes as part of the Shinto religion.

Today, there is a Shinto shrine in almost every village, town, and suburb in Japan. The shrines are easily identified by their distinctive gate, called a *torii* (taw-ree). Cleanliness is very important in the Shinto religion, so visitors wash their hands and mouth before approaching the shrine. People visit their local shrine to celebrate the new year and to ask the gods for help in difficult times. Shinto also plays an important role in life cycle events, such as birth, coming-of-age, and wedding ceremonies.

Above: **People may worship in the privacy of their homes. This image of a cat with one raised paw is placed on a Shinto table to bring good luck to its owner.**

Buddhism

Buddhism was introduced to the Japanese royal court in A.D. 552. It became popular with the masses in the thirteenth century. Buddhism did not replace Shintoism but was practiced alongside it.

Christianity

Christianity was introduced to Japan in the sixteenth century. It was banned during the period of national isolation, and many Christians were persecuted for their beliefs. Japan's Christian population has remained constant at about 1 percent.

Left: **This Great Buddha sits in Kamakura. Buddhism teaches that human suffering is due to craving and desires, and that meditation to eliminate these desires can lead to spiritual enlightenment. Buddhists also believe in reincarnation — that when a person dies, his or her soul is reborn into another living form. Buddhist beliefs have had a great influence on Japanese attitudes toward life and death. Because Buddhism has a positive concept of death, most Japanese funerals are Buddhist.**

Language and Literature

Spoken Japanese

The Japanese language developed over thousands of years. The sounds of the spoken language are simple, and its grammar is logical and regular. Although Japanese grammar is not difficult to master, the spoken language has many subtleties that take time to learn. Children begin by using a simple, rough form of the language. As they grow older, they learn more polite forms of speech. They also learn to speak indirectly, using suggestions rather than making bold statements, which are considered rude.

Left: Reading is a good way to pass the time. To read a newspaper, you need to know about three thousand written characters, or kanji!

COMICS IN JAPAN

In Japan, reading comic books, known as *manga* (mahn-gah), is a popular way for people to relax and escape from the pressures of everyday life. So, it is not surprising that manga publishing is a massive industry in Japan — about two billion manga are printed each year.

(A Closer Look, page 52)

Written Japanese

Early Japanese had no writing system. In the sixth century, Chinese characters, called *kanji* (kahn-jee), were adopted as the official written language of educated Japanese noblemen and Buddhist monks. Shortly after kanji was introduced to Japan, the characters were adapted into a simplified writing system, called *hiragana* (hee-rah-gah-nah), which was used by women. A third system, called *katakana* (kah-tah-kah-nah), was also developed. Today, all three systems of writing are used in written Japanese.

Literature

Japan has a rich literary heritage. The earliest surviving work, the *Kojiki* (*Record of Ancient Matters*), dates from A.D. 712. This collection of ancient myths includes early examples of Japanese poetry. The first Japanese novels were written by women in the Heian era. The *Genji Monogatari* (*The Tale of Genji*), written by Murasaki Shikibu, is one of the greatest works of Japanese literature. In the twentieth century, two Japanese novelists, Kawabata Yasunari and Oe Kenzaburo, have been awarded the Nobel Prize for literature.

Above: Japan has a huge publishing industry, printing more novels per person than any other country. Romances, thrillers, detective stories, and historical novels sell millions of copies each year. Poetry is also very popular.

Arts

Crafts

Traditional crafts suffered a decline in the early twentieth century. Many people were interested in using only new and modern objects. Today, people are rediscovering the work of craftspeople, such as potters, papermakers, and woodworkers. Craft museums preserve and display traditional crafts, and traditional skills are being recognized in Japan and abroad. Skilled artists are called "living national treasures." These men and women receive money from the government to teach their skills to others and keep the traditional crafts alive.

The Japanese have created pottery objects since prehistoric times, and Japan still produces some of the best pottery in the world. Beautiful pottery can be seen even in ordinary households. Lacquered objects are created by covering wood with many layers of sap from the lacquer tree. This sap gives the objects a hard, smooth surface that can last for thousands of years. Lacquer is used to make household objects, such as lunchboxes and trays.

Below: **Japanese artists produce textiles, wooden furniture, paper, dolls, swords, bamboo objects, kites, masks, and musical instruments. Here are some examples of how colorful and vibrant Japanese crafts can be.**

Painting

In the past, paintings documented everyday life and the passing seasons. A single scroll depicting flowers, birds, or other seasonal topics was kept in the main room of the house and changed several times a year. Many people still observe this custom.

Calligraphy

Calligraphy is the art of writing Japanese characters with a brush and ink. Calligraphy may be used to enhance a painting, or the characters may stand alone with just one or more large characters on a scroll. Students study calligraphy at school, learning how to write graceful, balanced characters using the correct brush strokes.

Prints

Woodblock printing is one of the best-known Japanese arts. Colorful, bold prints are made by carving a picture into wood, applying ink, and then pressing the wood onto paper. Woodblock prints became popular in the eighteenth century among the merchant classes in Edo (Tokyo). Woodblock prints were brought to Europe and had a great influence on European artists, such as Vincent Van Gogh. However, not all Japanese artists create traditional paintings or prints. Japan has a thriving modern art scene with artists producing all types of artwork.

KIMONOS

A traditional Japanese form of dress is the kimono. There are different types of kimonos for different occasions. They can be worn for weddings or even around the house. While a kimono is very beautiful to look at, wearing it properly can be rather tricky.
(A Closer Look, page 60)

Traditional Theater

In Japanese theater, the actors convey action and emotion through stylized forms and symbolism. The same stories are retold many times, so the audience often knows the plot in advance. In traditional theater, all the characters are played by men.

Noh

One of the oldest theatrical forms is *noh* (NO). Noh plays are based on Shinto dances and Buddhist teachings, and the stories deal with moral issues. The stage is very simple. The actors wear masks and ornate costumes and move in a slow, stylized manner. A subtle movement of the hand or head may indicate that the character is crying, or happy, or angry. The dialogue consists of chanted, old-fashioned phrases that are impossible for modern Japanese to understand.

Bunraku

Bunraku (boon-rah-koo) combines storytelling, puppetry, and music. The puppets are about 4 feet (1.2 meters) tall and very skillfully constructed.

Above: **Masks used in Noh theater.**

Kabuki

Kabuki (kah-boo-kee) is a spectacular theatrical form that flourished during the Edo period. Kabuki is very enjoyable to watch, with colorful costumes, singing, dancing, and lots of action. The plots and acting style are melodramatic — women change into men, and lovers commit suicide.

Musical Accompaniment

All traditional theater forms are accompanied by musical instruments, including drums, flutes, and *shamisen* (shah-mee-sen), a three-stringed guitar. Other instruments include the *koto* (ko-to), a thirteen-stringed instrument.

Film, Television, and Popular Music

In addition to traditional arts, Japan produces movies, television programs, and popular music. These popular arts combine Western forms with Japanese content and artistic style. Japan's best-known filmmakers include Kurosawa Akira (*The Seven Samurai*) and Itami Juzo (*Tampopo*). Television programs follow familiar formats, such as soap operas.

Opposite: In bunraku, the stories deal with serious, adult themes, and the puppets can convey deep emotions. Their eyes, eyebrows, and mouths can move, and the puppeteers can make them climb a ladder or even open a lock.

Below: Pop stars sing catchy love songs and have huge fan clubs, just like in the West. Here, an aspiring pop star sings her heart out.

Leisure and Festivals

Ikebana

Ikebana (ee-keh-bah-nah), the art of flower arranging, is particularly popular with women. Students of ikebana learn to arrange flowers, leaves, and branches into a pleasing and harmonious display.

Tea Ceremony

The tea ceremony is the ancient ritual of serving green tea to guests. This is no ordinary cup of tea — the ceremony may last for up to four hours! The tea ceremony takes place in a quiet, peaceful setting, such as a small tea house in a garden. There are strict rules about how the tea is prepared. The tea ceremony teaches participants to appreciate simplicity and harmony with nature.

Cooking

Along with ikebana and the tea ceremony, cooking is one of the three arts considered essential for a new bride. Classes in Western cooking styles, especially French cuisine, are increasingly popular.

Below: **There are different styles of ikebana — some are modern, while others are traditional and more conservative.**

Left: Pachinko **(pah-cheen-ko) is a pinball game played with small steel balls in a slot machine. Pachinko parlors crammed with rows of machines can be found in every suburban area. Pachinko enthusiasts sit at the machines for hours, feeding in balls and hoping to win a prize. The game is very noisy — the balls make a noise that sounds like** *pachin!*, **hence the name "pachinko."**

Karaoke

Karaoke (kah-rah-oh-keh), singing along to prerecorded instrumental music, is hugely popular in Japan. The singer sings into a microphone and reads the lyrics on a television screen, while music plays in the background. Thousands of bars and karaoke clubs cater to people who come along with their friends for a night of singing and drinking.

Travel

The Japanese are avid travelers, not only internationally, but within their own country as well. On weekends and holidays, they enjoy traveling to hot springs, historical sites, and famous gardens.

Baseball

Baseball, or *besuboru* (beh-soo-baw-roo), was introduced from the West and is the most popular team sport in Japan.

The sport is played at all levels, from elementary school and high school to adult social clubs and the major leagues. Fifteen million people attend games each year. There are two major leagues, each with six teams. The team with the largest following is the Tokyo Giants. The top baseball players are treated as stars, the same as in the United States. This is not surprising, considering that Japanese adults and children enjoy playing and watching sports.

SUMO

Sumo wrestling has been practiced for fifteen hundred years. It is the oldest sport in Japan. Two large men weighing up to 594 pounds (270 kilograms) try to throw each other to the ground or out of a small dirt ring. Most Japanese enjoy sumo as spectators rather than participants, but some schools and universities have student clubs for wrestlers of all sizes, big or small.

(*A Closer Look, page 66*)

Left: **A youngster from the little league tries to perfect his batting stance. Watch him grip that bat!**

Golf

Golf is another popular sport. Because golf courses take up so much land, golf is considered a luxury sport. Joining a club is very expensive. Some companies pay for their managers' golf club memberships, so they can entertain business guests by taking them golfing. In cities where land is very limited, golfers practice at rooftop putting centers and at driving ranges with huge nets to stop the balls from flying into nearby buildings.

Soccer

Japan's first professional soccer league, the J-League, was established in 1993. The sport quickly became the latest trend among young, fashion-conscious Japanese. Shops were filled with J-League clothes, J-League phonecards, even J-League curry!

Martial Arts

Karate (kah-rah-teh) and *judo* (joo-doh) are modern sports that have evolved from traditional Japanese fighting and self-defense skills. These sports are unarmed martial arts that use punching, kicking, and throwing techniques to defeat an opponent.

Above: Kendo (ken-doh) **is fencing with bamboo swords. It is based on the sword fighting techniques used by samurai hundreds of years ago. All students, both boys and girls, study judo or kendo in junior high school, and there are many clubs for people of all ages. These students from a junior high school are putting on their gear.**

New Year's Day

New Year, or *Shogatsu* (shaw-gah-tsoo), is the biggest festival of the year. In preparation for the New Year, houses are cleaned and decorated. People visit temples and shrines on New Year's Eve and the homes of relatives and friends on New Year's Day. The first three days of the New Year are public holidays. In the past, pickled foods were eaten on these days so women could have a rest from cooking. Today, most people eat these dishes only on New Year's Day, and they buy them from the supermarket!

Gion Matsuri

One of Japan's most spectacular festivals, the *Gion Matsuri* (gee-on mah-tsoo-ree), is held in Kyoto on July 17. The first Gion Matsuri was held in A.D. 876. A plague was sweeping across the country, so the people of Kyoto held a parade to ask the gods for protection. Today, the festival is just an excuse to bring out the floats, celebrate Kyoto's history, and have a party. From 9 a.m. until 11 a.m., twenty-nine floats are carried or pulled through the town. The floats are decorated with carvings, gold leaf, tapestries, gongs, flutes, and drums. The atmosphere is lively and colorful and everybody enjoys themselves.

Above: **These musicians are playing flutes while riding on a float at the Gion Matsuri.**

38

Children's Day

May 5 is Children's Day, *Kodomo-no-hi* (koh-doh-moh-no-hee), a national holiday. This festival used to be called Boy's Day. Its traditions began as a way of wishing boys health and courage.

Bon Festival

The *Bon* (BON) festival is held in August. Originally, people offered prayers and performed dances in the month when ghosts were believed to return to Earth. Today, candles and lanterns are floated on rivers and lakes to guide the ghosts back to heaven or hell. Drum towers are set up in villages and towns, and hundreds of ordinary people perform a simple dance that goes on for hours. Many return to their home town to visit and clean their family grave, so all the train tickets are sold out in advance.

Left: This shop is selling banners for Children's Day. Paper or cloth banners shaped like carp, which are fish, are set up on bamboo poles outside family homes. Families fly the banners in the hope that their children will grow up to be as brave and strong as carp.

Food

Japanese Meals

The traditional Japanese diet is very healthy, consisting mainly of rice, fish, and vegetables. The staple food is rice. Most Japanese eat rice at least twice a day. Because rice is so important in the Japanese diet, the daily meals are called *asagohan* (ah-sah-go-han), or "morning rice;" *hirugohan* (hee-roo-go-han), or "noon rice;" and *bangohan* (ban-go-han), or "evening rice." Japanese dishes contain few spices. This allows the natural taste of the ingredients to come through. Many foods are eaten raw or lightly cooked, so only the freshest ingredients are used. A typical breakfast consists of rice, grilled fish, miso soup (a salty soup made from fermented soy beans), pickled vegetables, and green tea. A Western-style breakfast of toast, eggs, and coffee is also popular, partly because it is quicker and easier to prepare.

For lunch, many people visit small shops selling noodles, rice with curry gravy, or *sushi* (soo-shee). Sushi are bite-sized portions of vinegared rice topped with raw fish, seafood, or egg. Workers,

SUSHI

Sushi is very popular in Japan. Sushi toppings include tuna and caviar. Sushi can be made at home or bought from shops. It is expensive to purchase sushi from restaurants. "Rotating sushi" shops are a cheaper alternative.
(A Closer Look, page 68)

Left: The presentation of Japanese food is as important as its taste. Food is beautifully arranged on small individual dishes and decorated with carved vegetables or other garnishes.

students, and travelers enjoy convenient lunch boxes packed with small servings of rice, vegetables, meat, or fish. Western foods, such as hamburgers, pizza, pancakes, and spaghetti are also popular, especially among young people.

Dinner usually consists of rice with a number of dishes served on small individual plates — perhaps pickled or steamed vegetables; *sashimi* (sah-shee-mee), sliced raw fish; seaweed; *tofu* (toh-foo), bean curd; or *tempura* (tem-poo-rah), deep-fried seafood or vegetables. In the winter, many families enjoy meat, vegetables, and soups cooked in a pot at the table.

Above: **Although rice is the staple food in Japan, noodles are also popular. These children are trying out spaghetti.**

Influences from Other Countries

Over the centuries, dishes from various cultures have been introduced into Japanese cuisine. *Gyoza* (gyaw-zah), pork dumplings, came from China; *yakiniku* (yah-kee-nee-koo), grilled meats, came from Korea; and curry rice is a sweet, mild version of Indian curry. These dishes were adapted to suit Japanese tastes. Western foods are also changed to suit Japanese tastes; hamburgers and salads are eaten with Japanese sauces, and pizza is topped with seaweed and squid.

41

A CLOSER LOOK AT JAPAN

Let's now take a closer look at interesting aspects of Japan's history, culture, and society. Japanese arts and traditions have been around for hundreds, or even thousands, of years. Today, they are still enjoyed by Japanese people. You will learn more about these arts and traditions, such as architecture, gardens, wearing kimonos, and sumo wrestling. Etiquette is very important in Japanese society. Baths and hot springs, comics, and sushi are uniquely Japanese and provide an insight into how the Japanese live and play. You will also be introduced to some unusual gadgets created to solve the problems of Japanese life.

Opposite: **Festivals in Japan are colorful, energetic, and exciting. Children enjoy them as well, especially this duo beating a drum!**

Below: **These two children are sitting in a carrying box, waiting for their ride to start.**

Other topics in this section deal with important social issues. These include the impact of the bombing of Hiroshima and Nagasaki in World War II; the changing role of women in Japanese society; Japan's native people, the Ainu; and the yakuza of Japan's criminal underworld. Japan's rapid growth has resulted in environmental problems, such as water and air pollution. At the same time, natural disasters, such as earthquakes, volcanoes, and typhoons have caused great destruction in Japan.

Ainu, the Native People of Japan

The Ainu are the indigenous people of Japan. They lived in Japan before immigrants arrived from mainland Asia. The immigrants became the dominant group in Japan — the ethnic Japanese. The Ainu had to move north, and, today, most Ainu live in Hokkaido.

The Ainu have a unique culture with their own religious beliefs, social organization, festivals, and ceremonies. The Ainu also have their own artistic heritage. They have a rich oral tradition of epic poetry and produce beautiful textiles, often dyed with indigo and embroidered with distinctive designs.

For many centuries, the Ainu were forced from their land and persecuted by the ethnic Japanese. In the Meiji era, the government thought the Ainu should become like other Japanese. They introduced the "Former Native Protection Law" in 1899. This law gave the Ainu small farms if they agreed to give up

Below: **A Bear Festival ritual in progress. The bear was particularly important in Ainu beliefs. Bears were captured at a young age and raised in the village as special members of the community.**

A SPEECH IN AINU

In 1992, Kayano Shigeru, the first Ainu member of the National Diet, made a speech in the Diet on behalf of the Ainu people. The speech was in both Japanese and Ainu and was the first speech in Ainu ever to be recorded in the official record of the Diet.

Left: In Ainu Kotan Village, Hokkaido, the Ainu's woodcarving skills are demonstrated by their elaborate totem poles.

hunting and stay in one place. The government set up schools for Ainu children, where they were taught Japanese language, history, and culture. The teaching of Ainu language, history, and culture was banned. Today, only a few old people speak the Ainu language.

Despite their unique culture, the Ainu are not recognized as a separate ethnic group by the Japanese government. Many Ainu report that they are discriminated against by other Japanese. Recently, the Ainu have tried to save their culture and claim their rights as a unique ethnic group. A school in Hokkaido teaches the Ainu language to young Ainu. The Ainu want laws to be reformed so they can perform their traditional festivals. They also want the "Former Native Protection Law" to be replaced by a new law, the "Ainu New Law," which would be written by the Ainu.

Architecture in Japan

Traditional Houses

Japan's traditional buildings are beautiful, simple, and functional. Traditional houses can still be found in the countryside and sometimes in the cities. They are usually single-storied rectangular structures built of wood. Roofs are made of tiles or a thick layer of straw. This style of building is designed to withstand earthquakes and typhoons. If the building is destroyed, the materials used for construction make it easy to rebuild; however, these materials also make houses vulnerable to fire.

Unlike Western buildings, which have solid interior walls, traditional Japanese houses have sliding screens that divide the inside of the house into rooms. Some of these screens are thick and opaque, while others are made of translucent white ricepaper pasted onto a wooden grid. The moveable walls allow the interior of the house to be used flexibly. Rooms can be enlarged or divided, depending on need. Traditionally, the Japanese used little furniture. By day, a room might contain a low table and

Below: **This is an example of a wooden building in Kyoto.**

cushions to sit on; at night the living space would become a bedroom. Bedding was taken out of a large cupboard and laid out on the floor. Decorations were kept to a minimum. This style of living was simple, flexible, and uncluttered.

Shrines and Temples

The Japanese have also built distinctive public buildings, such as temples and shrines. Shinto shrines are simple wooden structures, often with only one room inside. They are usually set in a peaceful garden setting. There are no ornate statues and no figures representing gods. In fact, in early times, the Shinto religion had no buildings at all. People worshiped at sacred trees and rocks marked off by straw ropes hung with strips of paper.

In contrast, Buddhist architecture is more complex and ornate. Temples often consist of several structures: a pagoda, a large hall, sometimes a lecture hall, and living quarters for monks and nuns. Horyuji, a temple in Nara, is the oldest structure in Japan. It was built between A.D. 601 and 607 and was rebuilt in 670 after a fire. Nara is also home to the largest wooden structure in the world, the Great Buddha Hall of Todaiji.

Above: **Himeji Castle dates back to the sixteenth century. Many fortified castles were built by feudal lords during the sixteenth and seventeenth centuries. They are made of stone and have barred windows, gates, trapdoors, and spaces for firing guns and arrows. The main citadel is surrounded by barracks, kitchens, stables, and women's quarters, which are, in turn, surrounded by thick walls. If the castle came under siege, the lord would retreat to the top level of the citadel while his samurai fought below to protect him.**

Atomic Bombs

By August 1945, in World War II, the battle between Japan and the Allied forces had been raging for nearly four years. Many people feared that the war would drag on for a long time, causing many more deaths. The United States decided to try to end the war quickly by using a new weapon — the atomic bomb.

On the morning of August 6, an American plane flew over the city of Hiroshima and dropped an atomic bomb nicknamed "Little Boy." Little Boy generated an enormous amount of air pressure, heat, and atomic radiation. The heat burned everything in its path, including people. Three days later, a second atomic bomb was dropped on Nagasaki. After the bombing of Nagasaki, Japan surrendered.

The radiation generated had terrible long-term effects. More than 210,000 people had died by the end of the year. Many others died later from illnesses caused by the radiation. Some people were unable to have children, or had malformed babies.

Below: **The "A" Bomb Dome in Hiroshima is what is left of the building located at the place over which the atom bomb exploded. Great damage was caused by the strong wind generated by the bomb, and most of the houses and buildings within 1.5 miles (2.4 km) of the blast were destroyed.**

Sadako

At Hiroshima Peace Park, there is a statue of a young girl holding a golden crane. Around the statue are thousands of folded paper cranes, placed there by people from all over the world. This statue remembers all the children who were killed by the atomic bomb. It was inspired by a courageous girl called Sasaki Sadako.

Sadako was two years old when the atomic bomb was dropped on Hiroshima. Nine years later, she was diagnosed as having leukemia, a form of cancer caused by exposure to the atomic radiation. Sadako's best friend told her about an old Japanese legend that said anyone who folds 1,000 paper cranes will be granted a wish. Sadako hoped she would get well again and folded 644 cranes before she died in 1955, at the age of twelve.

Inspired by Sadako's courage and strength, her classmates folded the remaining 356 cranes and published a book of her letters. They started a project to build a monument for children killed by the bomb. Young people all over Japan collected money for the project. The statue was unveiled in 1958. At the bottom of the statue, a wish is inscribed: "This is our cry, This is our prayer, Peace in the world."

Above: School children gather at a memorial in Hiroshima. The bombing is remembered with particular horror because a single weapon was used to kill so many people. Most now agree that countries should work together to ensure that atomic weapons are never used again.

Baths and Hot Springs

The Importance of Cleanliness

Cleanliness is very important in Japanese culture. Both Shinto and Buddhist rituals use water for purification. For example, worshipers wash their hands and mouths before approaching a Shinto shrine. Cleanliness is associated with goodness and beauty. In fact, the Japanese use the same word for "clean" and "pretty"— *kirei* (kee-ray). Dirtiness is associated with evil; therefore, the Japanese take bathing very seriously. Bathing is a ritual to be enjoyed with family and friends, both at home and in public baths and hot springs.

A Japanese person would never step into a bath without washing first. A good scrub with a rough cloth and soap is followed by plenty of water to wash away the suds. This thorough wash is performed while sitting on a low stool next to the bath. Japanese bathrooms are designed to get wet, so there is no need to worry about splashing water around. After washing all the soap and dirt away, the person gets into the bath to soak. Baths are usually small but deep; the water goes right up to the neck. The bath water is very hot. After one member of the family finishes bathing, the next person bathes in the same clean water.

Above: **There are few people who enjoy a good bath as much as the Japanese. This woman enjoys both the water and the cool serenity of her environment.**

Today, most people have baths in their homes, but personal baths were once a luxury. Common people paid a small fee to bathe in communal baths, called *sento* (sen-toh). Sento are less popular than they used to be, but there are still about 1,650 sento in Tokyo alone. Most sento are divided into men's and women's sections, although there are some sento where men and women bathe together.

Hot springs, or *onsen* (on-sen), are even more popular than sento. Hot springs occur when water is heated underground by volcanic forces before rising to the surface of the earth. This supply of naturally heated water is channeled into baths. Hotels, gardens, and other facilities are built around the onsen to attract visitors. Visitors sit in the bath and enjoy the view, even in winter.

Left: **The Japan Onsen Association lists 2,500 hot spring areas in Japan, and there are over fifteen thousand onsen resorts. These two people are admiring the hot water at Noboribetsu Onsen in Hokkaido.**

Comics in Japan

In Japan, comics are known as *manga* (mahn-gah). There are different types for different readers. The biggest selling manga are *shonen manga* (shaw-nen mahn-gah), boys' comics, and *shojo manga* (shaw-joh mahn-gah), girls' comics. The biggest selling boys' manga, *Shonen Jump*, sells over four million copies in a good week. These manga are inexpensive, and they are often as big as telephone books! Their covers are colorful and glossy, but the inside pages are printed in black ink on cheap, rough paper. Each manga contains up to fifteen stories. Some of the stories are serialized — the story is revealed bit by bit in each issue, like a television series. Some stories relate to everyday life at school and home, while others are humorous stories or jokes.

Adults have their own comic books, although they also read boys' and girls' manga. There are manga that specialize in topics such as sports, romance, historical dramas, religion, war stories, and science fiction. The content and artistic styles vary greatly, from extreme violence to starry-eyed romance.

Below: **Reading manga is a popular way for Japanese men, women, and children to rest their minds and just relax.**

Ideas and Innovative Techniques

Manga artists and publishers are constantly trying out new ideas. A magazine that is not popular will quickly disappear from the stands. A big hit will bring huge sales, fame for the artist, publication in book form, and, perhaps, a television series based on the manga. The popular manga *Doraemon*, a comedy tale about a robot cat, started out in a children's manga magazine in 1970. It has now been published as a paperback series with dozens of books selling millions of copies, and it has also been made into an animated television show. The popularity of *Doraemon* has flowed over into toys, stationery, and other merchandise. Some television programs based on manga have even been exported to North America — for example, *Astro Boy* (called *Tetsuan Atom* in Japan) by the great manga artist Tezuka Osamu.

The best Japanese artists use innovative visual techniques to portray movement, emotion, and drama. The text may be part of the design, rather than being placed in speech bubbles. Like a movie, frames may jump from sweeping landscapes to extreme close-ups. A scene can be shown from any angle — from above or below, from across the street, or through the eyes of a character.

Above: **About two billion manga are printed each year! Japanese artistic techniques have had a great influence on comic book artists and animators around the world.**

Etiquette

Bowing

Politeness and proper behavior are very important in Japan. From the time they start school, children learn Japanese etiquette — the correct way to behave in particular social situations. Bowing is one aspect of etiquette. When Japanese people meet each other, they usually bow. If the person is a friend or coworker, they might just smile and nod their head or bow slightly. In formal situations, such as greeting a guest or customer for the first time, the bow is very low. Nowadays, many businessmen shake hands, and young people may prefer to just wave to their friends.

Exchanging Name Cards

Another important part of meeting someone for the first time is the exchange of name cards. All business people, many students, and some housewives have their own name cards. Cards are given whenever people meet someone new in a work or social situation. When exchanging name cards, the name card must be handed over with both hands, studied carefully, and then placed on the table or put away carefully. It is considered very rude to write on someone else's business card or to stick it in your back pocket.

Left: **When exchanging name cards, proper etiquette, such as using both hands, must be observed. A name card shows the person's name, title, workplace or school, and address. Some people have double-sided cards with Japanese printed on one side and English on the other.**

Above: **At a gathering, this woman arriving bows to the group she is meeting.**

Giving Gifts

When visiting someone's house, people will always bring a small gift. Gifts are also given in summer (mid-July to mid-August) and in winter (December). The gifts are beautifully wrapped with several layers of paper. When they go on a trip, travelers bring back presents for their friends, family, and coworkers. It would be considered rude to come back empty-handed, especially if the traveler had previously received presents from other people. Receiving a present means that you must return the favor when you get a chance.

Etiquette at Home

When entering a house, people remove their shoes and change into slippers. Different slippers are worn in the bathroom, and no slippers are worn on tatami floors. There are rules related to eating — for example, chopsticks should not be crossed or stuck upright in the rice, because these positions resemble an offering to the dead. Soy sauce should not be poured directly onto the rice; instead, small pieces of food should be dipped gently into a small dish of sauce.

Gardens

Different Styles

The Japanese have a unique tradition of landscape gardening. Gardens are carefully designed to enhance the natural beauty of a site and to create a peaceful and harmonious environment. There are many different types of Japanese gardens, each with its own traditions and style. In natural gardens, water is an important part of the landscape, forming pools and streams. Paths wind through the gardens, and bridges or stepping stones cross the streams.
Stone lanterns may be placed by pathways. Trees, such as pines and Japanese maples, are trimmed into graceful shapes. Some plants are featured for their seasonal displays — plum and cherry trees for their blossoms, maples for their vibrant autumn leaves. Ferns and moss soften the rocks and banks. There are few straight lines or obvious patterns — no rows of trees or flower beds and few lawns. The effect is natural and controlled at the same time. These simple and beautiful gardens are often found near Japanese temples.

Below: **This is a view of Ginkakuji Garden in Kyoto. It is an example of how exquisitely beautiful gardens can be.**

Some Japanese gardens use no plants at all. Sand and stones are arranged like islands in a sea, and the sand is raked in flowing patterns around the stones. This style of garden is very dramatic, with its contrasting tones of white sand and dark stones. The most famous stone garden is found at Ryoanji, a Zen temple in Kyoto. A wooden viewing platform looks out onto the garden. The viewer sits on the platform and quietly contemplates the garden's beauty.

Another characteristic of Japanese gardens is the "borrowed view." Sometimes a building, tree, or mountain can be seen from the garden. Instead of ignoring this feature or seeing it as an intrusion, the gardener places trees and other objects in a way that includes and frames it, making it "part" of the garden.

Above: **The stones in this garden in Kyoto are carefully raked into beautiful patterns. The swirling pattern might be used to suggest the sea.**

Bonsai

Most Japanese gardens are small, so they are designed to show nature on a small scale. Another way the Japanese do this is by growing *bonsai* (bon-sye), or miniature trees. Some bonsai are only a few inches high. They are created by trimming their branches closely to control their growth.

Inventions

"Capsule" Hotels

With so many people living in such a small place, the Japanese are always looking for ways to make life easier and more convenient. People around the world are familiar with Japan's small, handy electronic products, such as Walkmans, miniature televisions, and tiny mobile phones. However, some Japanese inventions are a little more unusual.

After entertaining business guests in the city, many businesspeople find that they have missed the last train home. Hotels are expensive, so where do they spend the night? This problem was solved by the invention of "capsule" hotels. Instead of sleeping in a room with a bed, each guest has his or her own capsule — a plastic box about 4 feet (122 cm) wide, 4 feet (122 cm) high, and 6 feet (2 m) deep. The capsules are stacked along a wall, so dozens of guests can sleep in a small building. Each capsule has a tiny television, a light, an alarm clock, and a small shelf for personal belongings. When it is time to go to sleep, the guest simply pulls a sliding cover over the open end of the capsule.

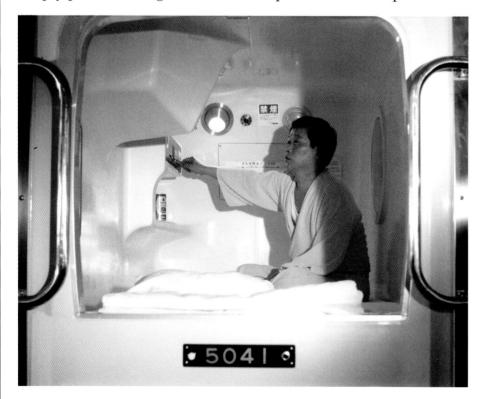

Left: **A guest settles down for the night in his capsule. The hotel supplies pajamas, and clothes and luggage are stored in lockers.**

"Pet" Chicks

For animal lovers living in small city apartments, a toy manufacturer invented the Tamagotchi — an electronic "pet" that fits on a key ring! The Tamagotchi is an egg-shaped toy with a small screen, like a computer game or a digital watch. ("Tamagotchi" is a combination of the Japanese words for "egg" and "watch.") The screen shows a chick that must be cared for by the owner. At certain times of the day, the owner must press buttons to feed, clean, and play with the chick. If the chick is neglected, it will become sick and eventually die. Tamagotchi owners take their pets very seriously, pressing buttons to see to their needs.

Pop Culture and Everyday Life

There are many other inventions designed to improve everyday life. Inventing gadgets has become part of Japanese popular culture, with people competing to see who can come up with the wackiest idea. Many gadgets never make it to the mass market, but if an idea is clever enough, it might become very popular.

Kimonos

Modern Japanese wear jeans, T-shirts, suits, dresses, and skirts. However, on special occasions they are sure to bring out their most beautiful *kimono* (kee-mo-no).

A kimono is a long robe made of silk, cotton, or synthetic materials, bound with a wide sash called an *obi* (oh-bee). The basic shape of a kimono is always the same, so kimono fabric is precut and rolled into standard lengths. Nearly all kimonos are the same size, regardless of the wearer. The fabrics come in virtually all colors and a wide range of designs. When buying a kimono, the most important things to consider are the color and quality of the fabric.

Left: Children also wear kimonos. Isn't this girl's kimono a gorgeous, brilliant red? She has a yellow and red obi tied in a bow behind her.

YUKATA

In summer, heavy formal kimonos are put aside, and both men and women wear light, cotton kimonos called *yukata* (yoo-kah-tah). Brilliantly colored yukata are worn at summer parties, while simple, dark blue and white yukata are worn at home. On hot, humid evenings, there is nothing nicer than sitting around in a cool yukata with friends, drinking iced tea and eating watermelon.

Different types of kimonos are worn on different occasions. On New Year's Day or at a wedding, young unmarried women wear brightly colored kimonos with long sleeves that hang almost to the ground. Married women wear elegant black, formal kimonos with white, gold, and silver decorations on the lower portion.

Above: **This bride, with her large, white headdress, is wearing the special white bridal kimono. This multilayered kimono is complicated to wear, and it takes several people to help the bride get dressed.**

Wearing a Kimono

Wearing a formal silk kimono is quite an effort. Under the kimono is a cotton robe, waist padding to make the body look fashionably flat, and a series of belts to hold everything in place. The outer kimono goes on top, and then the long obi is wrapped around the body and secured. The skirt is bound tightly, so the wearer must walk with small steps. There are special schools to teach women how to select and wear kimonos.

Men's Clothing

On formal occasions, Japanese men wear shorter kimonos over wide, pleated trousers called *hakama* (hah-kah-mah). The most common colors for men's clothing are black, blue, and gray.

Natural Disasters

Earthquakes

Earthquakes are caused by pressure beneath Earth's crust. Earth's surface is made up of a number of huge sheets of rock that are about 43 miles (70 km) thick. Most of the time, these plates shift position very slightly, but sometimes they move violently, causing earthquakes.

The islands of Japan are located where several of these plates meet. This makes the country particularly prone to earthquakes. Tremors (small earthquakes) are very common. The Japanese are used to dealing with these tremors, which make windows rattle and buildings sway. Major earthquakes, however, are extremely destructive. The worst earthquake in modern Japanese history occurred in 1923. The Great Kanto Earthquake, centered in the Kanto Plain, devastated the Tokyo area, and over one hundred thousand people died. Scientists are trying to reduce earthquake damage by studying ways to predict earthquakes and by constructing buildings that are more resistant to earthquakes.

Below: **This is how destructive an earthquake can be. Not only is property badly damaged; many lives are lost as well.**

Typhoons

Japan is also exposed to typhoons, which are strong tropical storms that bring destructive winds and heavy rainfall. Every summer and fall, dozens of typhoons develop over the Pacific Ocean, and some of them hit the east coast of Japan. Many weaker typhoons just bring heavy rain without doing any serious damage. However, when a strong typhoon hits a settlement, it destroys buildings and causes flooding.

Dealing with Disasters

Although major earthquakes, volcanic eruptions, and typhoons are infrequent, most local governments have emergency plans to deal with disasters. These plans outline the steps that should be taken if a major earthquake or typhoon hits, including traffic control and evacuation of residents. Schools and workplaces hold evacuation drills so people will know what to do if a fire breaks out. Certain areas, such as parks and squares, are designated as safe areas, and local residents are required to know how to get to the nearest safe area. In case disaster strikes, some families keep a stock of essential supplies, such as drinking water and dried food.

Above: Japan has eighty-three active volcanoes. The Asu volcano is one of them. Volcanic eruptions occur when the heat, gas, and molten rock beneath Earth's plates build up pressure and erupt through Earth's surface. There are several volcanic eruptions in Japan every year.

Pollution

The Air and Water

Pollution of the air, rivers, and seas was a major problem in the early stages of Japan's economic growth. There were no environmental laws, so factories simply dumped industrial waste or flushed it out to sea. One of the worst environmental disasters occurred in the town of Minamata during the 1950s. A chemical factory emptied mercury waste into the river and sea, poisoning the fish and shellfish. The people who ate these animals also were poisoned. Thousands of people were affected. Many people died, and others gave birth to children with severe birth defects.

In 1967, Japan introduced the "Basic Law for Environmental Control." Four years later, the Environmental Agency was set up to promote environmental protection. Companies were required to meet new environmental standards and develop technologies to reduce pollution. The Japanese have also been active in

Below: **Japan's rapid industrialization since the 1960s brought economic prosperity and a high standard of living to its people. However, this growth also caused damage to the environment. Today, regulations control the amount of air pollution emitted by factories.**

demanding better pollution controls. Public and official efforts have helped reduce the amount of pollution produced by Japanese industries. Efforts are being made to regulate the exhaust emissions from cars, buses, and trucks; to introduce vehicles that run on electricity or low pollutant fuels; and to develop devices that remove the dust and sulfur from smoke emitted by factories.

Dealing with Garbage

Japan has a major problem with garbage. Consumer products are wrapped in many layers of packaging, which end up as a mountain of refuse. Every person in Japan throws out over 2.2 pounds (1 kilogram) of household refuse every day, and factories and construction sites also produce a great deal of waste. There are few spaces for landfill, so some of the refuse is burned. Another way of dealing with the garbage problem is to use the waste to create new land. Areas of the sea are closed off, drained, filled with garbage, and topped with soil. Much of the land along Tokyo Bay has been reclaimed from the sea as part of a national effort to ensure that economic prosperity is not achieved at the cost of the environment.

Above: **Government and civic groups promote recycling of newspapers, cans, and bottles. All refuse has to be separated into "burnable" and "non-burnable" garbage. Even public trash cans come in pairs. Here, there are three sets of garbage cans—for burnable rubbish, non-burnable rubbish, and recyclable bottles and cans.**

Sumo Wrestling

Sumo (soo-moh) originated as a Shinto ritual about fifteen hundred years ago. Sumo wrestling bouts were performed at temples, and were dedicated to the gods with prayers for a bountiful harvest. Sumo was later introduced to the royal court. Rules were formulated and techniques were developed. Over time, sumo, which was previously a rough-and-tumble affair, became more like the sumo of today.

Present day sumo is a combination of sport and ritual. The sumo ring is about 15 feet (4.6 m) in diameter and is made of a hard clay surface covered with a thin layer of sand. The sumo bout often lasts less than thirty seconds. Before each round the wrestlers perform a series of warming up rituals. They toss a handful of salt on the ground (to purify the soil), advance to the center of the ring, get into the starting position, and stare at each other menacingly before returning to their side of the ring. They perform this ritual four times before the fight begins.

Below: **It sometimes seems as if the wrestlers are just pushing and shoving each other, but there are many techniques and skills that the wrestlers must learn. Every move and technique has a name. There are over seventy ways for a wrestler to be forced out of the ring!**

Left: **There are six Grand Tournaments each year — three in Tokyo and one each in Osaka, Nagoya, and Kyushu. Think how hard these sumo wrestlers must train to be fit for competition. Besides that, to gain their huge size, they need to eat special diets consisting of large quantities of thick rice porridge and beer. These are sumo wrestlers wearing yukatas on a break from training.**

Winning a Bout

To win a bout, the sumo wrestler must force his opponent out of the ring or throw him to the ground. A bout is lost if any part of the body, except the soles of the feet, touches the ground. The wrestler is not allowed to punch his opponent, pull his hair, attack his eyes, choke him, or kick his stomach or chest.

Champion Wrestlers

Grand champions must not only be great wrestlers; they must also show the dignity and personal qualities expected of a sumo champion and of a representative of Japan. Some of the biggest wrestlers are actually Hawaiian, although they take Japanese wrestling names. The Hawaiian wrestler Akebono was the first non-Japanese wrestler to reach the level of grand champion.

Sushi

What is Sushi?

Sushi is one of Japan's most popular dishes. Most types of sushi consist of a small mound of vinegared rice with a piece of raw fish on top and a dab of Japanese horseradish in between.

Preparing Sushi

To Westerners, the idea of eating raw fish is not very appealing. Most people imagine that the fish will be smelly and slimy.

Below: **This selection of sushi certainly looks like it could tempt a few taste buds! It includes raw tuna, fish eggs, shrimp, and egg.**

However, sushi is never smelly, because the fish is extremely fresh. Sushi chefs visit the fish market every morning to buy fresh fish caught during the night. The fish is not slimy but quite firm and smooth, and the taste is subtle. Only the best pieces of fish are served to the diner; the rest is discarded. The fish must be cut with the proper technique so that it looks and tastes just right. Even the rice is special — it must be delicately flavored with vinegar, sugar, and salt. Due to the level of skill involved, becoming a sushi chef takes years of dedicated training.

Having Your Sushi and Eating It, Too

The most popular sushi toppings are tuna, mackerel, prawns, squid, octopus, eel, and shellfish. Sushi is eaten by holding it with chopsticks or fingers, dipping it in soy sauce, and eating it in one bite. Along with the sushi, the diner eats pieces of pickled ginger and drinks green tea, beer, or *sake* (sah-keh), rice wine.

Since sushi is difficult and time-consuming to prepare, most people go out to restaurants to enjoy it. Customers sit on stools at a counter, and the chefs work on the other side of the counter. The sushi ingredients are displayed in a glass case that runs along the center of the counter. Each serving consists of two pieces of sushi

on a small plate. The atmosphere is lively, with customers and chefs chatting and calling out orders.

Most sushi restaurants are expensive, but there is a cheaper option — "rotating sushi" shops. In these shops, plates of sushi are placed on a conveyor belt that runs around the counter. The customer sits at the counter and chooses plates of sushi as they go by. Different types of sushi have different colored plates to indicate their price. At the end of the meal, the staff simply count the plates and add up the bill!

Above: **These chefs working in a sushi bar in Japan are preparing sushi for their hungry customers. See how skillful they are with their knives.**

Women in Japan

History of Japanese Women

During the Heian era, women enjoyed a period of intellectual freedom and produced some of the great works of Japanese literature. However, their freedom was curtailed during the feudal era, when women were considered subordinate to men. The history of Japanese women reached a low point in the Tokugawa period. Women were confined to their homes and made completely dependent on men. The only other alternative was the life of the *geisha* (gay-shah), a woman who was trained in music, dance, singing, and conversation. Geisha were paid to entertain men and were looked down upon by others.

Reforms for Women

The reforms of the Meiji era brought new opportunities for women. They were allowed to divorce, inherit property, own and manage land, and act as the head of a household. However, these rights were limited. The feminist movement in the early 1900s saw the extension of limited political rights to women, but

Below: Two out of five workers are women, but their average pay is half that of men. Even if a woman manages to get a job in a large firm, she has poor prospects for promotion, because it is assumed that she will soon leave to marry and have children. Women are generally expected to resign as soon as they get married.

women did not achieve the right to vote in national elections until 1946, during the American occupation. Other laws were reformed to grant women equal rights in inheritance, marriage, and custody of children. In practice, however, the old traditions were slow to change. Equal opportunity guidelines were introduced only in 1985, and they are not legally enforceable.

Above: **This cheerful woman is tending to her food stall at Tsukiji market in Tokyo.**

Women's Achievements

Despite these challenges, women have made their mark in virtually every aspect of Japanese society. In 1986, Doi Takako became the first woman to chair the country's largest opposition party, the Socialist Democratic Party. Kuroyanagi Tetsuko has been voted Japan's most popular television personality for five years running and is also a famous writer, conservationist, and social worker. In 1975, in celebration of the International Year of Women, a team of Japanese women became the first all-woman team to scale Mount Everest. Japanese women have always had strength, creativity, and endurance; today they are bringing these qualities into the public arena.

Yakuza

Organized Crime in Japan

The *yakuza* (ya-koo-za) dominate organized crime in Japan. They are criminal groups that can be compared to the Mafia. They are involved in drug smuggling, prostitution, gambling, political payoffs, violent crime, and other criminal activities.

Code of Honor

The yakuza's organizational structure is based on the family. At the top is the *Oyabun* (oh-yah-boon), or "father," who has absolute authority in the group. The lower members, called *kobun* (koh-boon), or children, must serve the Oyabun. A typical family of yakuza has twenty to two hundred members. Since a strong kobun may have his own subfamily, a yakuza clan may have over one thousand members. The largest and most powerful clan is the Yamaguchi clan, based in Kobe. Most clans tolerate each other and respect territorial boundaries, but, from time to time, clans fight for control of territories or businesses.

Below: **All yakuza members are men. The only woman involved in the work of the clan is the Oyabun's wife. Yakuza believe that women are weak and incapable of loyalty, so women are not trusted with clan secrets.**

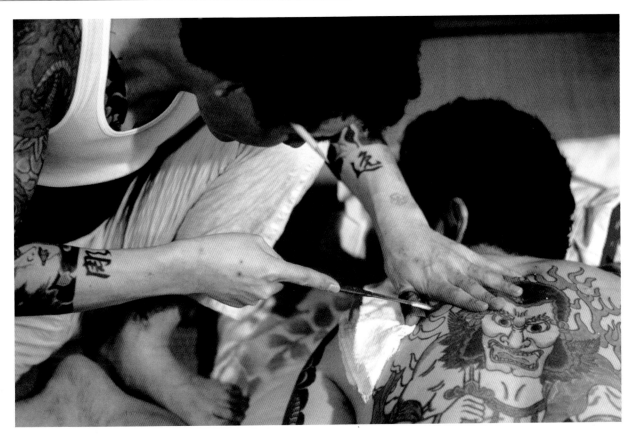

Yakuza have a code of honor that originates in samurai traditions. Their code calls for loyalty to the clan and unquestioning obedience to the Oyabun. Yakuza clans have formal ceremonies and rituals for initiating, rewarding, or punishing clan members.

Previously, the yakuza were considered noble. They made money from crime but helped ordinary people. Even in modern times, the yakuza have provided public service and aid. After the Kobe earthquake in 1995, yakuza members provided aid to injured and homeless people long before the Japanese government did. Nonetheless, this positive side of the yakuza is overshadowed by their criminal behavior. In recent years, several members of the public have been killed by the yakuza. Most people fear and avoid them.

Above: **One of the ways in which yakuza members can be identified is by the tattoos they wear. The tattoos are inscribed with bamboo needles dipped in ink, and a full body tattoo may take over one hundred hours to complete. Tattooing is considered an art form in Japan. Traditional designs include images of demons, dragons, flowers, clouds, and women.**

Dealing with the Yakuza

In 1992, the Japanese government introduced a law to restrict the activities of the yakuza. In order to avoid these controls, the yakuza use an elaborate system of fronts, including businesses, religious organizations, and sports clubs.

RELATIONS WITH NORTH AMERICA

Relations between North America and Japan have experienced ups and downs since the nineteenth century. The first official contact was initiated by the Americans, who forced Japan to trade with the West in 1854. In the following decades, Japan strove to learn Western technologies, but there was limited human exchange between the two regions.

Around the turn of the century, many Japanese settled in the United States and Canada. Some faced discrimination in their new country, and tensions peaked when Japan went to war against the United States and Canada in 1941. The war tainted relations between Japan and the United States for many years.

Opposite: **Young Japanese are quick to pick up on the latest sporting trends, such as in-line skating, surfing, snowboarding, and soccer. The most important thing is wearing the right gear!**

Below: **Mickey and Minnie Mouse wear Japanese attire!**

During the post-war U.S. occupation of Japan, relations between Japan and North America improved. The Americans introduced a democratic constitution, legal reforms, and American popular culture. With the growth of Japan as an economic power, economic and defense relations have been strengthened. Japan and North America also have rich cultural ties. There are now large, established Japanese-American and Japanese-Canadian communities, as well as a North American community in Japan.

Beginnings of Trade with Japan

Official North American relations with Japan had an abrupt start in 1854, when the United States sent ships to force Japan to trade with the West. Unable to compete with the superior technology of Commodore Matthew Perry's iron "Black Ships," the Japanese opened their ports to Western traders for the first time in over two hundred and fifty years. In the following decades, the Japanese government pursued an energetic policy of learning about Western ideas and technologies, while retaining Japanese cultural identity. Although North American teachers and missionaries spent time in Japan, direct contact between Japanese and North Americans was limited.

Japanese Migration

In the 1890s, large numbers of Japanese farmers lost their land because they were unable to pay heavy taxes. In search of a better economic future, thousands of Japanese emigrated to the United States and Canada, particularly to Hawaii and the Pacific coast. By 1910, there were tens of thousands of Japanese in North America. North Americans knew little about Japan and held

Below: **General Douglas MacArthur led the Allied occupation of Japan after World War II, holding the position of Supreme Commander for Allied Powers. He held this post until 1951.**

strong prejudices against Asians. Many people feared that the Japanese immigrants would take their jobs. A series of laws were enacted to restrict Japanese immigration and Japanese immigrants from owning land or becoming U.S. or Canadian citizens.

Bombing of Pearl Harbor

The Japanese bombing of Pearl Harbor in the U.S. Hawaiian Islands in December 1941, during World War II, produced anti-Japanese feelings. People of Japanese descent who had lived their whole lives in America were suspected of spying for Japan. Over a hundred and twenty thousand people were forcibly moved into internment camps for the duration of the war. Many Japanese-Americans and Japanese-Canadians proved their loyalty to their new country by enlisting in the armed forces. Japanese-American soldiers served as interpreters in the Pacific and fought in combat units in Europe. They earned many medals for their heroism.

Above: **When Commodore Matthew Perry arrived in Japan, he made an offer the Japanese could not refuse.**

American Occupation of Japan

Japan surrendered to the Allied forces in August 1945, and American forces took control of the country. The Americans reformed Japan's constitution, system of government, and legal structure. The new constitution guaranteed democratic government and freedom of speech and religion. It gave workers the right to organize unions and women the right to vote. Land laws were reformed so that more people would be able to own land. The emperor was forced to state publicly that he was not a god. This was the first time the Japanese people had ever heard the emperor's voice. The Japanese also discovered American popular culture, brought in by American soldiers and sailors. The American occupation built a strong foundation for trade, defense, and cultural ties between North America and Japan. This relationship continues today.

Current Relations

Current relations between Japan and North America are shaped by shared economic and defense interests in the Pacific region. Japan, the United States, and Canada are strong trading and defense partners. However, trade and defense policies sometimes cause conflicts between the countries.

WAR HEROES

The Japanese-American 442nd military unit accomplished one of the most celebrated missions of World War II in 1944. Three hundred American soldiers were trapped by German forces. The 442nd unit went to rescue them and, in half an hour of intense fighting, broke through German lines, although losing over half its men in the fight. The men of the 442nd were hailed as heroes throughout the U.S. when they returned.

Economic Ties

The United States, Canada, and Japan are major world economies. Japan buys raw materials from the United States and Canada and exports manufactured goods, especially machinery, motor vehicles, and electronic products. The United States buys about 30 percent of Japanese exports and is Japan's largest trading partner. Japanese brands, such as Sony, Canon, Toyota, and Honda, are a common sight in North America.

In recent years, trade between Japan and North America has been in Japan's favor — Japan sells more goods to North America than it buys. Japan has a huge trade surplus — it exports much more than it imports. The United States and Canada, on the other hand, owe money to Japan for their imports.

At times, Japan has been accused of "dumping" products on the U.S. and Canadian markets. Many Americans and Canadians fear that the flood of cheap imports is damaging local industries and causing North Americans to lose their jobs. They also accuse Japan of protecting its own market by restricting the entry of foreign goods. Japan and its trading partners meet regularly to discuss fair trading practices.

Below: **Mazda and other Japanese cars are popular in the United States.**

U.S. Military Presence in Japan

Japan and the United States have maintained a close defense relationship since the U.S. occupation of Japan. Japan allows the United States to maintain military bases on Japanese soil. This increases U.S. influence in Eastern Asia and gives the United States a strategic position from which to monitor activities in Russia, China, and North Korea. In exchange, the United States is committed to protecting Japan and promoting stability among the East Asian countries. There are almost fifty thousand U.S. troops stationed at military bases throughout Japan, including Yokosuka near Yokohama, Iwakuni on southern Honshu, and Okinawa. Today, many Japanese are questioning the need for so many U.S. troops in Japan. Since the breakup of the Soviet Union, some people feel that a strong U.S. presence in Japan is no longer necessary. On the other hand, others observe China's nuclear tests and increasing naval strength and argue that U.S. troops offer Japan greater security. In 1995, the rape of an Okinawan schoolgirl by U.S. military personnel caused public outrage and contributed to the heated debate about this issue.

Above: A U.S. soldier stands in salute at the gate of Kadena Air Base, located in central Okinawa.

Cultural Connections

Walk down the streets of a Japanese city, and you will soon see evidence of North America's impact on Japanese popular culture. Almost everyone wears Western clothes. Young people have a particularly American sense of style. Boys favor jeans, baggy pants, baseball caps, and T-shirts with English slogans. Girls wear jeans, T-shirts, and short skirts. American labels — or Japanese labels with American-sounding names — are popular.

Above: **Another American cultural export to Japan — there is now a Tokyo Disneyland.**

Enjoying American Culture

Young Japanese like to eat North American foods. City streets are lined with American fast-food restaurants, including McDonald's and Shakey's Pizza. The Japanese also have their own fast-food restaurants such as Mos Burger, which introduced burgers with Japanese sauces. The success of the Japanese burger forced McDonald's to introduce burgers designed for Japanese tastes. Beer has replaced sake as the preferred alcoholic drink. American influence can be seen in many popular pastimes; for example, Japan's favorite sport is baseball. Many Japanese bands and pop stars are modeled after American performers.

Japanese Influence on American Culture

The transfer of culture is not all one-way. Japanese comic books have a large following in Japan and have greatly influenced on American comic books and animation. Japanese animated television series and movies are dubbed with English voices and released in North America.

On the sports scene, Japanese martial arts, such as karate and judo are widely practiced in the United States and Canada. Martial arts films are flourishing in the United States, and Japanese culture has been popularized in such films as *The Karate Kid*. North Americans can enjoy Japanese cuisine at the many Japanese restaurants in urban areas. Californians have even exported their own style of sushi back to Japan. The "California roll" contains avocado, cooked crab, and mayonnaise instead of raw fish. Tourism and education have also contributed to cultural exchanges between Japan and North America. Every year, almost five million Japanese visit the United States, making it Japan's top tourist destination. In 1995, the United States was the most popular study destination for Japanese students.

GODZILLA

Japanese animated television series and movies are dubbed with English voices and released in North America. Many people do not even realize that characters such as the Power Rangers and Godzilla originated in Japan!

Below: **Over five hundred thousand North Americans visit Japan each year. Here is one visitor enjoying a flower-viewing party with his friends.**

Japanese in North America

The United States has the world's largest Japanese population living outside Japan, with about 260,000 Japanese and Japanese-American residents. About 37 percent of overseas Japanese live in the United States. Canada ranks fourth, with 25,000 people of Japanese descent.

The First Generation

When the Japanese first came to North America in the late 1890s, they were escaping extreme poverty in their homeland. In the United States, they had to work long hours in poorly paid jobs as farm laborers and domestic workers. In Hawaii, Japanese worked in the sugarcane fields. Working and living conditions were harsh. Despite these many difficulties, they were able to save money to buy cheap, unwanted land. Through skill and hard work, the Japanese tended the land until it became fertile. By 1920, one-sixth of California's crops were grown by people of Japanese descent.

The Japanese who traveled from Japan to North America called themselves the *issei* (iss-say) — the first generation. Once they became settled, many men wrote back to Japan and asked friends or family members to arrange a marriage and send the bride to America. Like their husbands, these women hoped to return to Japan some day, but as they formed families and established roots in America, returning to Japan became difficult.

NEW FAMILIES

Japanese men living in America found wives from back home by exchanging photographs in the mail. These new brides were called "picture brides."

Left: **Although they remain Japanese in appearance, the third generation, or sansei, are culturally closer to mainstream America than they are to traditional Japanese culture. This Japanese-American girl is fluent in English and goes to school with other American children.**

The Second Generation

The issei faced language problems and discrimination, so they established their own businesses, churches, and temples. Their children, the *nisei* (nee-say), second generation, worked alongside their parents on family farms or in businesses and attended the local schools with non-Japanese children. They preserved their culture by attending Japanese language school on Saturday and participating in traditional festivals. The nisei were American citizens by birth and were the first generation to call America home.

During World War II, the Japanese community suffered greatly as families were moved to internment camps. Houses and businesses had to be abandoned or sold. After the war, the nisei worked hard to rebuild their homes and businesses and provide a better life for their children, the *sansei* (sahn-say), third generation.

The Third Generation

Many of the sansei are now adults and have their own children, the fourth generation of Japanese-Americans and Japanese-Canadians. Many live in the suburbs rather than in traditional Japanese neighborhoods. In some cities, Japanese cultural organizations have been established to teach Japanese traditions.

Above: **Due to the government policy of multiculturalism in Canada, these Japanese-Canadians are encouraged to keep their culture and customs alive.**

North Americans in Japan

The foreign population in Japan has been growing steadily over the past several years. At the end of 1995, there were 1.4 million registered foreign residents in Japan. Of these, over 43,000 (3.2 percent) were from the United States, which makes Americans the fifth most populous group of foreigners in Japan. Canadians make up less than 1 percent of Japan's foreign population.

Many North Americans come to Japan to work because salaries in Japan are high by American standards. The most common job for native English speakers is teaching English at

home or at language schools or high schools. As more people learn Japanese, opportunities are opening up in other areas, including banking and finance, law, science, and publishing.

Foreigners in Japan have to cope with language problems, the high cost of living, and different customs and social expectations. In the larger cities, some foreign residents spend much of their time with other foreigners. Although this makes it easier to cope in the short term, they never adapt to the Japanese way of life. Others learn the language and try to fit into Japanese society. Those who settle in Japan permanently usually become fluent in Japanese and gain a deeper understanding of Japanese culture.

Above: **North Americans and other foreigners come to Japan for many reasons. Some come to study Japanese at private schools or universities. Others are interested in particular aspects of Japanese culture, such as art or religion. Here, students are learning Japanese at a language school in Tokyo.**

Exchange Programs

There are many organizations in Japan and North America that run cultural exchange programs. These organizations facilitate exchange by providing scholarships and research funding, arranging special visas or introductions, and holding classes in Japanese language and culture.

The Japanese government encourages foreign students to study in Japan by offering scholarships. There are currently about seven thousand students receiving government scholarships in Japan. Another form of exchange is the Working Holiday Scheme

Below: **The Japanese have a keen interest in Western culture. These people are learning English at a community class in Japan.**

run by the Japanese and Canadian governments. Young Japanese and Canadians are given special six-month visas that allow them to work and travel in each other's country. The Japanese government operates the JET (Japan Exchange and Teaching) program, which employs native English speakers in Japanese schools. The government also runs the Japan Foundation, a cultural exchange organization that is part of the Ministry of Foreign Affairs. There are dozens of private organizations all over Japan, the United States, and Canada that promote good relations between Japan and North America. They hold a variety of events to link the Japanese and North American communities.

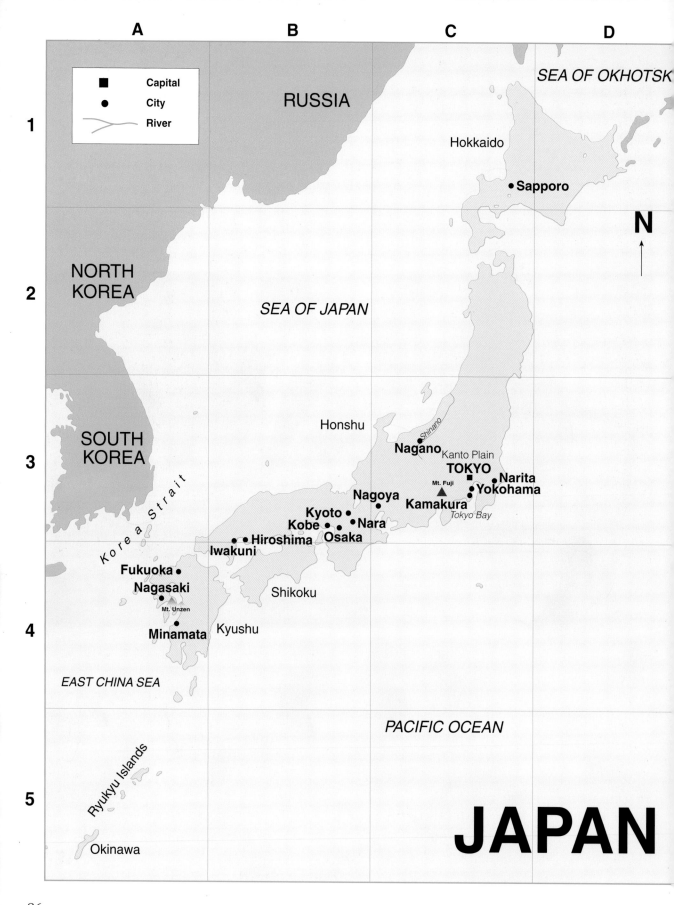

Above: The majestic splendor of Mount Fuji.

East China Sea A4

Fukuoka A4

Hiroshima B3
Hokkaido C1
Honshu C2

Iwakuni B3

Kamakura C3
Kanto Plain C3
Kobe B3
Korea Strait A3
Kyoto B3
Kyushu B4

Minamata A4
Mount Fuji C3

Mount Unzen A4

Nagasaki A4
Nagano C3
Nagoya C3
Nara B3
Narita C3
North Korea A2

Okinawa A5
Osaka B3

Pacific Ocean C5

Russia B1
Ryukyu Islands A5

Sapporo C1
Sea of Japan B2

Sea of Okhotsk D1
Shikoku B4
Shinano C3
South Korea A3

Tokyo C3
Tokyo Bay C3

Yokohama C3

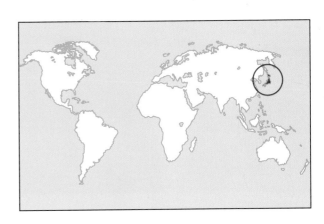

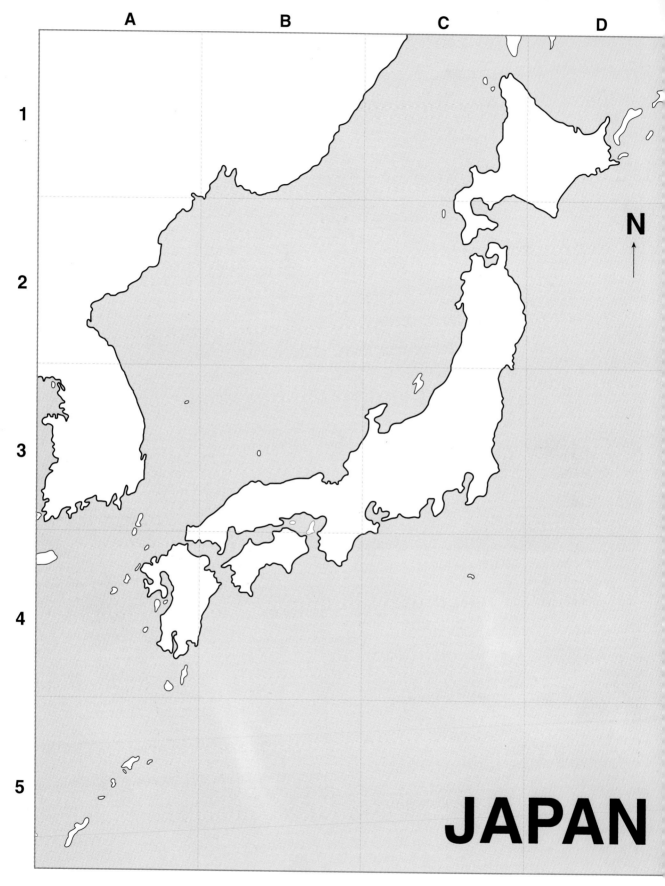

JAPAN

How Is Your Geography?

Learning to identify the main geographical areas and points of a country can be challenging. Although it may seem difficult at first to memorize the location and spelling of major cities or the names of mountain ranges, rivers, deserts, lakes, and other prominent physical features, the end result of this effort can be very rewarding. Places you previously did not know existed will suddenly come to life when referred to in world news, whether in newspapers, television reports, or other books and reference sources. This knowledge will make you feel a bit closer to the rest of the world, with its fascinating variety of cultures and physical geographies.

Used in a classroom setting, the instructor can make duplicates of this map using a copy machine (PLEASE DO NOT WRITE IN THIS BOOK!). Students can then fill in any requested information on their individual map copies. Used one-on-one, the student can also make copies of the map on a copy machine and use them as a study tool. The student can practice identifying place names and geographical features on his or her own.

Above: **The cool serenity of a torii.**

Japan at a Glance

Country Name	Japan (Nihon)
Flag	White with a large red circle (representing the sun) in the center
Land Area	144,651 square miles (374,650 square kilometers)
Largest Islands	Honshu, Hokkaido, Kyushu, Shikoku
Capital	Tokyo
Other Major Cities	Yokohama, Osaka, Nagoya, Kyoto
Highest Mountain	Mount Fuji at 12,388 feet (3,776 meters)
Population	125 million
Ethnic Groups	Japanese and Ainu (99.2 percent), Korean (0.6 percent), others (0.2 percent)
Life Expectancy	76.6 years (male), 82.7 years (female)
Language	Japanese
Literacy	99 percent of people aged fifteen years and over can read and write
Major Religions	Buddhism, Shinto
Important Festivals	New Year's Day, Children's Day, Bon
Major Exports	Manufactured products, including machinery, motor vehicles, and consumer electronics
Major Imports	Manufactured products, fossil fuels, food, and raw materials
National Bird	Pheasant
National Flower	Cherry blossom
Imperial Crest	Chrysanthemum
National Anthem	*Kimigayo*, "The Reign of the Emperor"
Currency	Japanese yen (¥125 = U.S. $1 as of 1998)

Opposite: **Children in Okinawa pose with their favorite hero.**

Glossary

Japanese Words

Ainu (eye-noo): the original inhabitants of Japan.

besuboru (beh-soo-baw-roo): baseball.

bonsai (bon-sye): miniature plant.

bunraku (boon-rah-koo): traditional puppet theater.

futon (foo-ton): bedding.

geisha (gay-shah): a woman paid to entertain men with traditional singing, dancing, and conversation.

gyoza (gyaw-zah): fried pork dumplings.

hiragana (hee-rah-gah-nah): Japanese phonetic alphabet, used for Japanese words and grammar.

ikebana (ee-keh-bah-nah): the art of flower arranging.

issei (iss-say): the first generation of Japanese immigrants in North America.

kabuki (kah-boo-kee): form of classical theater.

kanji (kahn-jee): Japanese written characters that originated in China.

karaoke (kah-rah-oh-keh): singing to recorded music.

katakana (kah-tah-kah-nah): Japanese phonetic alphabet.

kendo (ken-doh): Japanese fencing with bamboo swords.

kimono (kee-mo-no): traditional robe.

koto (ko-to): thirteen-stringed musical instrument.

manga (mahn-gah): comic books.

nisei (nee-say): second-generation Japanese-Americans and Japanese-Canadians, children of the issei.

noh (no): form of classical theater.

obi (oh-bee): a wide sash tied around the waist. It is worn with a kimono.

onsen (on-sen): hot springs.

pachinko (pah-cheen-ko): a type of pinball game.

sake (sah-keh): rice wine.

sansei (sahn-say): third-generation Japanese-Americans and Japanese-Canadians.

sashimi (sah-shee-mee): sliced raw fish.

sento (sen-toh): public baths.

shogun (sho-gen): military leader.

sumo (soo-mo): traditional form of wrestling.

sushi (soo-shee): raw fish or seafood on a bite-sized mound of vinegared rice.

tatami (tah-tah-mee): smooth floor mats made from woven rice stalks.

tofu (toh-foo): bean curd.

torii (taw-ree): gateway at the entrance of a Shinto shrine.

yakiniku (yah-kee-nee-koo): meat grilled on a hot plate, Korean-style.

English Vocabulary

abstract art: art that makes use of shapes and patterns, rather than showing things as they really are.

adapted: changed to suit a different purpose.

aggression: offensive violation.

avid: extremely keen and enthusiastic.

avoid: keep from coming into contact with.

conflicts: serious differences between parties about important issues.

cuisine: way of preparing food that is typical of a certain country.

cultural identity: a person's sense of who he or she is, based on the beliefs and behavior of the social group to which he or she belongs.

dedicated: extremely committed.

destruction: tremendous wreckage and damage.

dialogue: conversation.

endurance: stamina in the face of hardship and difficulty.

evacuation: the removal of persons or things from a place for safety reasons.

exotic: a way of describing something interesting, unusual, or even strange, from a country far away.

fashion-conscious: being aware of the latest fashion trends and keeping up with them.

formats: methods of presentation.

fortified: strengthened, usually with stone or other durable materials.

functional: useful and serving a purpose.

harmony: in smooth accordance with; a lack of disturbance or conflict.

inaccessible: very difficult or impossible to reach or obtain.

indigenous people: people who are natives of a land.

industrial waste: garbage and other waste material produced by a factory.

innovations: new inventions or creations.

melodramatic: excessively emotional.

organizational structure: hierarchy of a group of people gathered together to achieve certain goals.

originates: begins or starts from.

ornate: elaborately decorated.

ousted: thrown out of power or government.

pilgrimage: a journey to a destination that is of personal significance, often for religious reasons.

plague: a widespread infection that causes serious illness and/or death.

prehistoric: before history was recorded.

presentation: display of items.

revolution: overthrowing established rulers by force. This is accomplished by the people being ruled.

rituals: ceremonies or practices.

rival: competitor who vies for the same goal.

skyscrapers: very tall buildings, located in the city, used mainly for business purposes.

specialize: to focus only on a particular topic at the exclusion of other areas.

spectacular: very impressive.

sprawling: spread out.

strategist: an expert in planning and directing large-scale military or political movements.

subtle: not obvious.

synthetic: made from chemical or artificial substances rather than natural fibers.

tattoos: designs, patterns, or marks on a person's skin. This is done by puncturing the person's skin with tiny holes and using dye to fill the holes.

tedious: lengthy and tiresome.

thriving: growing and developing.

unique: special, found in no other place.

virtually: practically.

vulnerable: prone to either physical or emotional wounds.

More Books to Read

Country Topics for Craft Projects. Richard Tames and Sheila Tames (Franklin Watts)

Discovering Japan. Deborah Tyler (Crestwood House)

Japan. Country Fact Files. John Baines (Raintree Steck-Vaughn Publishers)

Japan. Festivals of the World series. Susan McKay (Gareth Stevens)

Japan. People and Places series. Vincent Bunce (Franklin Watts)

The Japanese. Clare Doran (Thomson Learning)

The Japanese. The Ancient World series. Pamela Odijk (Silver Burdett Press)

Japanese Food and Drink. Lesley Downer (The Bookwright Press)

Origami Sculptures. John Montroll (Dover Publications)

Papercrafts Around the World. Phyllis Fiarotta and Noel Fiarotta (Sterling Publishing)

A Taste of Japan. Jenny Ridgewell (Thomson Learning)

Tokyo. Cities of the World series. Deborah Kent (Children's Press)

Women in Society: Japan. Elizabeth Kanematsu (Times Editions)

Videos

Faces of Japan. (Pacific Mountain Network)

Japan, the Island Empire. (International Video Network)

Japan: Tokyo to Taiwan. (International Video Network)

Kodo: Heartbeat Drummers of Japan. (Rhapsody Films)

Web Sites

www.jinjapan.org

sunsite.sut.ac.jp/asia/japan/

www.chowa.org

jin.jcic.or.jp/kidsweb/

www.sadako.org

Due to the dynamic nature of the Internet, some web sites stay current longer than others. To find additional web sites, use reliable search engines with one or more of the following keywords to help you locate information on Japan. Keywords: *Hiroshima, Japan, kimono, Mount Fuji, samurai, sushi.*

Index

agriculture 19
Ainu 20, 44, 45
Akebono 67
American occupation 77
animals
    Asiatic brown bear 9
    badgers 9
    cranes 9
    deer 9
    gulls 9
    Japanese macaque 9
    wild boars 9
architecture 46, 47
arts
    calligraphy 31
    crafts 30
    paintings 31
    woodblock prints 31
Astro Boy 53
atomic bomb 13, 48

baths 50
bonsai 57

Canada 6, 77, 78
"capsule" hotels 58
castles
    Himeji 10, 47
    Nagoya 10
    Osaka 10
champion wrestlers 67
cherry blossoms 9
children 22, 28
China 6, 10, 12, 13, 20
cities
    Hiroshima 13, 48
    Hokkaido 20, 44, 51
    Kamakura 11, 27
    Kobe 6
    Kyoto 6
    Kyushu 67
    Nagasaki 13, 48
    Nagoya 6, 67

Osaka 6, 21, 67
Tokyo 6, 15, 17, 21, 65
Yokohama 6, 21, 79
Yokosuka 79
clans
    Fujiwara 11
    Minamoto 11
    Yamato 10
cleanliness 26, 50
climate 8
comic books 28, 52
constitution 16
cooking 34
crime 16, 72, 73

Doraemon comics 53

earthquakes 7, 46, 62
economy 13, 18, 19
education
    cram schools 25
    elementary school 25
    examination hell 25
    high school 24
    homework 25
    school curriculum 25
    school year 25
    teachers 25
    university entrance 24
Emperor Akihito 16
Emperor Hirohito 13, 16
Emperor Meiji 12, 15
energy 19
environment 64, 65
Environmental Agency 64
etiquette
    bowing 54
    giving gifts 55
exchange programs
    Japan Foundation 85
    JET 85
    Working Holiday
        Scheme 85

festivals
    Bear Festival ritual 44
    Bon 39
    Children's Day 39
    Gion Matsuri 38
    New Year's Day 38
filmmakers
    Itami Juzo 33
    Kurosawa Akira 33
flag 5
food
    presentation 40
    sashimi 41
    sushi 40
    tempura 41
    tofu 41
    yakiniku 41
foreign population 84
futon 21

gardens 56, 57
geisha 70
government
    Diet 17
    Liberal Democratic Party
        17
    prefectures 17
    prime minister 16
Great Kanto Earthquake 62
group relationships
    family 22
    school 22

hakama 61
Hawaii 13, 76, 82
Heian era 11
Hiroshima 13, 48, 49
Hiroshima Peace Park 49
Horyuji temple 47
hot springs 50
houses 46

ikebana 34

individuality 22
islands
    Hokkaido 6, 20
    Honshu 6, 21, 79
    Kyushu 6
    Ryukyu 8
    Shikoku 6
issei 82

Japanese-Americans
    82, 83
Japanese-Canadians 83

karaoke 35
kimono 60, 61
    color 60
    fabric 60
    obi 60
    shape 60
Korea 6
Koreans 20

language
    grammar 28
    hiragana 29
    kanji 29
    katakana 29
literature
    Kojiki 29
    The Tale of Genji 15, 29

MacArthur, Douglas 76
manufactured goods 18
military bases 79
Minamoto Yoritomo 11, 15
modernization 15
Mount Fuji 7
musical instruments 33

nature 26
navy 12
nisei 83
nuclear power stations 19

pachinko 35
Pacific Ocean 6

Pearl Harbor 13, 77
Perry, Matthew 77
"picture brides" 82
police 17
pollution
    environmental protection
        64
    garbage 65
    Minamata 64
popular culture 80
population 20, 21

recycling 65
religion
    Buddhism 27
    Christianity 27
    Shinto 26, 47, 50
restaurants 69
rice 19, 40
Ryoanji 57

Sadako, Sasaki 49
sake 69
"salaryman" 23
sansei 83
seasons 8
Self Defense Force 12
shogun 11
Siberia 10
Sino-Japanese War 12
sports
    baseball 36
    judo 37, 81
    karate 37, 81
    kendo 37
    soccer 37
    sumo 66
sushi 68, 81

Tamagotchi 18, 59
tatami 21
tea ceremony 34
temples 47
theater
    Bunraku 32
    Kabuki 33

Noh 32
Todaiji temple 10
Tokugawa Ieyasu 11, 15
torii 26
trade 12, 78
travel 35
typhoons 63

United States 6, 48, 77, 78

volcanoes 63
voting 16

women
    achievements 71
    challenges 71
    creativity 71
    feminist movement 70
    feudal era 70
    Heian era 70
    household finances 23
    Meiji era 70
    self-enrichment 23
    social structures 23
    status 23
    Tokugawa period 70
    workers 70
World War II 13, 16, 77, 83
wrestlers 66, 67
writers
    Kawabata Yasunari 29
    Murasaki Shikibu 15
    Oe Kenzaburo 29

yakuza
    clans 72
    code of honor 73
    drug smuggling 72
    gambling 72
    kobun 72
    loyalty 72
    obedience 73
    organizational structure 72
    Oyabun 72
    prostitution 72
    tattoos 73